Balancing Work and Love

Also By Elaine Grudin Denholtz

PLAYS
Frozen
The Dungmen Are Coming
Hey Out There, Is Anyone Out There?
Some Men Are Good at That
The Highchairs
Love Games

FILMS
Summerhill
Waiting . . . The Life Styles of the Elderly
The Dental Auxiliary
What's Inside
Is That What You Want for Yourself?
Another Mother (Eugene O'Neill adaptation for television)

BOOKS
Education, Where It's Been, Where It's At, Where It's Going (contributor)
The Highchairs
How to Save Your Teeth and Your Money (co-author)
The Dental Facelift (co-author)
Having It Both Ways: A Report on Married Women with Lovers
Playing for High Stakes

BALANCING
Work & Love

JEWISH WOMEN FACING
THE FAMILY-CAREER
CHALLENGE

Elaine Grudin Denholtz

BRANDEIS UNIVERSITY PRESS

Published by University Press of New England   Hanover and London

BRANDEIS UNIVERSITY PRESS

Published by University Press of New England, Hanover, NH 03755

© 2000 by Brandeis Univesity Press

All rights reserved

Printed in the United States of America

5 4 3 2 1

Library of Congress Cataloging-in-Publication Data

Denholtz, Elaine.

Balancing work and love : Jewish women facing the family-career
challenge / by Elaine Grudin Denholtz.

    p.   cm.

Includes bibliographical references.

    ISBN 1–58465–000–1 (cloth : alk. paper) — ISBN 1–58465–001–X (pbk. :
alk. paper)

    1. Jewish families—United States. 2. Jews—United States—Social
conditions. 3. Working mothers—United States. 4. Work and
family—United States. I. Title.

HQ525.J4 D46   2000

306.85'089'924073–dc21   00–009416

To Mel and Peeps

and in memory of my mother

Lillian Sachs Grudin

Contents

Acknowledgments   ix

Introduction   1

1. Religious Women: *Rachel, Leah, Bernice, Aya*   7

2. Workaholics: *Erica, Beth*   28

3. Intermarriage: *Lauren, Susan*   45

4. Political Women: *Amy, Rona, Tracy*   61

5. Professional Volunteers: *Elinor, Rhoda, Sharon*   76

6. Married Women with Children: *Nancy, Cindy, Naomi*   91

7. Young Single Women: *Michelle, Jody, Lily*   108

8. Single Moms Raising Children Alone: *Marian, Barbara,*
   Karen, Wendy   124

9. Changing Goals, Reshuffling Priorities: *Roberta,*
   Fran, Monique   144

10. Career Conflicts, Women on the Cusp: *Rima, Debbi*   161

11. Assimilation, Feminism: *Natasha, Joan*   175

12. Conclusions   189

Bibliography for Further Reading   201

Acknowledgments

Conventional wisdom claims that writers live a lonely life and that a book is written painfully and alone. Perhaps this is true for some, to some extent. However, it was not my experience. I loved writing this book.

Along the way, I had the help and encouragement of many people: colleagues and librarians, researchers and professors, scholars and authors. I am grateful for their willingness to talk to me, to argue a point, and to provide information and support.

To Bracha Weisbarth at the Waldor Library, to the fast and courteous librarians at the Ruth Rockwood Memorial Library, to researchers at the Women's Resource Center of the National Council of Jewish Women and the Jewish Education Association, and to professors at Brandeis University, I owe a debt for their assistance. I was lucky to find them.

To my Scribblers group who listened each month to yet another interview and another chapter, I am grateful for their thoughtful comments and corrections.

To the International Research Institute on Jewish Women, which provided a generous grant for travel and transcriptions of my interview tapes, I offer genuine thanks.

And to Professor Steve Cameron, my colleague at Fairleigh Dickinson University, thanks for transforming my Wordstar floppies to Word. It's magic to me.

Above all, I was blessed with a dream editor, Phyllis Deutsch. Every page of this book was informed by her intellectual vigor and keen sensitivity to the material.

Without the women who shared their stories with me, who cried and laughed and touched old wounds, there would be no book. I can't name them because I promised I would not, but I hope they feel that I told their stories well. In the interview sections, I have included the exact words that were spoken. I am enriched for having met them.

To my family and friends, thanks for forgiving my inattentions and distractions. To Mel, who is always there for me, and to my father Peeps, whose music taught me to hear the beautiful sounds of words, my love and gratitude.

E.G.D.

Balancing Work and Love

INTRODUCTION

Like many contemporary women, I work out at a gym. Three days a week at 6:30 A.M. I arrive at the Women's Health Club of the Jewish Community Center (JCC) in New Jersey where I swim my mile, work out, and walk on the track.

While I rely on my routine to keep me physically fit, part of the pleasure is the women I have met. We chat easily. Whether we are talking over the buzz of the treadmills or applying blush at the makeup mirrors, we exchange anecdotes and stories.

Bound together as Jewish women, many of us talk about our jobs and about the pressures of working full time or part time. Or the kick we get out of doing volunteer work. Or the stress of changing jobs. Work, whatever the story, is a major topic of our conversations.

So is family, the people we love. We talk about our children's triumphs and our aging parents. The emotional pain of a divorce and the struggle to pay bills to repair a car or a broken heart.

At Fairleigh Dickinson University, where I teach in the English/Communications/Philosophy Department, conversations among academic women are not very different. Work and Love is a constant theme, an aria almost every woman sings as she faces the day-to-day challenge to get it right. American women, whether or not they are Jewish, have been forced into performing juggling acts. Indeed, the basic plotline women share has us performing a treacherous high-wire act every day as we try to meet the expectations of our jobs and the expectations of the people we love.

How did this happen? What transformed us?

Work!

American women went out to work in unprecedented numbers in the 1970s. As two working parents increasingly became the norm, work transformed our religious attitudes and restructured our family life. How families function today is largely built around the parents' jobs. And while Jewish women may say they never make choices at the expense of their families, they make adjustments and compromises as they peform the balancing act.

How are Jewish women different from Gentile working women? Is there a special experience we share as Jews that informs our decisions and guides us toward our work/love choices? Are we especially pressured by tenets peculiar to Judaism as a religion and as a culture?

The Old Testament is straightforward in explicating the priorities of Jewish women, exhorting us to be fruitful and multiply. It establishes our roles as mothers and wives, as keepers and transmitters of Jewish ritual and tradition within the family and across the generations. Marrying, bearing children, and tending to the family are crucial components of Jewish women's identity.

The Old Testament also offers women a template for behavior. Frowning upon idleness and pride, it extols the virtues of hard work and humility before husband and God. Proverbs 31, for example, in asking, "a virtuous woman, who can find?" urges women to "maketh linen garments and selleth them." A woman who "feareth the Lord, she shall be praised. . . . Give her of the fruit of her hands: and let her works praise her in the gates." A praiseworthy woman is one who creates and maintains a Jewish home for her husband and children, an activity enhanced by honest labor inside or outside the home. She achieves self-worth by giving of herself to others.

We do not know how well this biblical image of virtuous womanhood matched the lives of real women living in ancient times. We do know, however, that there are no biblical sound bites for Jewish women facing the twenty-first century. Contemporary Jewish women, well educated, intelligent, and assertive, have joined America's overworked workforce in droves. They grapple daily with dual Jewish imperatives, one ancient, one modern. Traditional Judaism emphasizes the centrality of mothering, while contemporary Judaism stresses achievement as doctors, lawyers, and professionals.

We've all seen these women, waiting with their children in doctors' offices, rushing to piano recitals or ball games, trying to carve out "quality time" with their families. We've seen them in trains and on planes, frantically tapping out work on their laptops, with briefcases full of work to do when the kids go to bed. In their personal lives are husbands and children, parents and siblings, lovers and friends, people they love and want to please. In their worklives, they face people they have to please: bosses and colleagues, co-workers and staff. Whether they are turning out ad copy or performing cardiac surgery, selling products or writing computer programs, women now answer to more voices than ever before. It is the confluence and the collision of these two imperatives that make us who we are. Not surprisingly, our anxiety and intensity are palpable. Can this conflict be resolved? What can be done when there are only twenty-four hours in a day?

I thought about this phenomenon for several months. Does being Jewish help us balance work and love? Or does it complicate those efforts? Is claiming "Jewish working woman" as a special category even valid? Many of the women I interviewed were involved in Hebrew school, Passover preparations, bar and bat mitzvah planning, synagogue activities, Jewish charities, and volunteer work. Some harbored an intense loyalty to Israel. They supported Jewish causes and maintained a Jewish outlook. Even the most secular Jewish women told me that being Jewish informed their lives.

As you read these interviews, you will hear what happens when contemporary Jewish women, raised with a heightened sense of what is possible in terms of education and work, try to heed time-honored injunctions to care for close-knit, stable Jewish families. You will see how American-based values of competition, individualism, and materialism impact the Jewish family, and you will witness the impact of Jewish values on political movements such as feminism. Indeed, in offering a close look at the issues facing Jewish working women today, this book offers a tantalizing glimpse of how much we've become like our Gentile neighbors and yet how we still remain apart.

Writers do a lot of brainstorming. We are probably annoying to our friends and colleagues when we are in the throes of "growing" a book. I make lists, I ask questions, I photocopy newspaper articles, and I badger my friends with questions. Then, once I think I'm onto something, everything changes. The subject inhabits me, it takes over like a dybbuk, and I am possessed. I know I must write that book.

Once I decided on the title "Balancing Work and Love," I began to speak purposefully to Jewish women I knew. Striving to be unobtrusive, I nonetheless asked numerous questions in order to get a feel for the subject.

Next, I tested my ideas on my support group of women writers. We call ourselves Scribblers. These are academic women, Jewish and Gentile, with whom I've met for a decade. Talking to them and reading them chapters throughout the writing process helped me to shape this book.

Armed with a long list of questions, I began speaking to women who are attorneys and physicians, entrepreneurs and marketers, teachers and consultants. This book includes the experiences of Jewish working women, wives and mothers, divorced and widowed women, single moms and professional volunteers (isn't it about time we defined this as work?), young singles and workaholics, political women and religious women. Despite this diversity, virtually every woman told me she does a balancing act every single day.

"I should be in the circus," one woman told me. "I juggle better than any clown. Then I hit the Maalox because I'm always in a rush, always stressed out. Forty-two on Maalox. Can you believe it?"

The interviewing process is the part I loved best. It took me about ten months to complete the interviews that provide the spine of the book. No interviewee was paid and each one took time out of her crazy schedule to fit me in. We met in offices, restaurants, kitchens, hotels, whatever worked out. Without these women, there would be no book. Because I promised them anonymity I can not name them, but they know who they are and I thank them for trusting me with their stories.

It was challenging to create appropriate categories for the interviews, and to group them into chapters. In some cases, an interview "fit" two or more chapters. For example, I might have placed Beth (in the Work-aholic chapter) in the chapter on intermarriage or even in the chapter on married women with children. But I tried to group women accord-ing to the most definitive aspect of their interviews, and Beth's super-charged workday seemed to take special precedence.

Every woman in this book is balancing work and love. It's the specif-ics that bring each individual to life. Because I want you to relate to these women and the stories they tell, I've emphasized their voices and kept quantitative analysis to a minimum. These are real women — our mothers, sisters, daughters, and friends. Some laughed, some cried. Every interview was different, a unique conversation. Most tapes, when transcibed, ran about fifty pages, often rambling and full of detours, with lots of starts and stops. Although I sometimes deleted bits of con-versation in the interest of clarity, I never changed any of their words. These women wanted me to get it right, to be clear, to tell what it feels like to be in their shoes.

Some of the women were wounded, all were generous, and many were resilient and unflinchingly honest. I like to think they felt com-fortable talking to me. I found them trustworthy and hope they found me trustworthy as well.

Every writer relies on research. In order to contextualize the inter-views with existing sociological studies, I had the help of many librar-ians. Like detectives, they dug out the material I needed to provide added significance to the interviews. The support of the Waldor Me-morial Library, Fairleigh Dickinson University, the Ruth Rockwood

Memorial Library, the Jewish Education Association, the Women's Resource Center and the Jewish Theological Seminary was invaluable.

Finally, I've provided a bibliography of books on Jewish working women and working women in general. I've read these books with pleasure and hope you'll want to browse further.

1

RELIGIOUS

WOMEN

RACHEL

LEAH

BERNICE

AYA

Ask little kindergarten girls: "What do you want to be when you grow up?"

In the 1950s, they answered "Mommy." "Teacher." "Princess." In the 1970s, the same question elicited a wider variety of responses: "Ballerina." "Nurse." "Movie star."

In the 1990s, little girls brought up by Jewish working women and feminists widened the net to include "Astronaut." "Doctor." "Consultant." Even if they didn't know what a consultant did, they knew mommy went to her office.

Now, entering the new millennium, we ask the question again.

One job you don't hear mentioned often is rabbi. Yet women rabbis in Conservative, Reform, and Reconstructionist synagogues have entered the job market, as have women cantors. Indeed these working women, often mothers raising children, are balancing work and love as *deeply religious* women.

Although women rabbis are unacceptable in Orthodox synagogues and other strictly observant groups, they are a growing presence, validated by their synagogues and appreciated by their congregants. Like astronauts landing on Mars, they have ventured into a new world outside their traditional orbit. Do they experience special conflicts? Is it a burden to be a deeply religious working woman? Does a spiritual commitment to Judaism make the work harder or easier?

Meet four devout women.

First, RACHEL, a Lubavitch mother of five.

Second, LEAH, a young mother and a Conservative rabbi, who heads a Jewish day school.

Third, BERNICE, also a rabbi, who leads a large Reconstructionist congregation in Pennsylvania.

And last, AYA, a young Orthodox mother living in Florida, whose singular goal is to move her family to Israel the moment she completes her Ph.D.

Most Jews and many non-Jews understand the differences among the three major American Jewish congregations. On the right is *Orthodox* Judaism, whose followers consider it to be the only authentic Judaism. Orthodox Jews follow strict laws for traditional behavior, require kosher homes, abstain from work on the sabbath, and forbid intermarriage.

On the left is *Reform* Judaism. Its adherents believe that many traditional practices are irrelevant to modern society. They emphasize social issues and do not view intermarriage as a sin.

In the middle is *Conservative* Judaism, a centrist point of view whose congregants may be kosher and traditional or closer to modern Reform Judaism.

So what is a *Lubavitch* and a *Reconstructionist*?

The Lubavitch are the largest group of Hassidim, who embrace an ultrapious version of Orthodox Judaism originating in Eastern Europe. In the United States the Lubavitch are best known for their outreach

programs to convert non-Orthodox Jews. Lubavitchers, fervently observant and pious, comprise only a small fraction of American Jews, far
less than the 470,000 Orthodox Jews identified by the 1990 National
Jewish Population Study.

Reconstructionism, a growing American phenomenon pioneered by
Rabbi Mordecai Kaplan in the 1920s, is regarded as the left wing of the
Conservative movement. It advocates equality for women and lay leadership in religious services. Reconstructionism does not impose sanc-
tions on rabbis who perform mixed marriages.

Rachel

RACHEL, 49, is a Lubavitch mother of five children ages 18, 17, 15, 14,
and 10. "I nursed them all and I never stopped working."

Self-employed, she started her own business producing videos and
print material for such Fortune 500 companies as Xerox, Marriott, and
AT&T. She is one smart woman, passionate and forthright. She invited
me into her sprawling suburban home, and we spoke across her ten-
foot dining-room table. She wore a long skirt and a loose, long-sleeved
overblouse. She had a curtain of silky, dark, shoulder-length hair.

"A wig?" I asked.

"Of course," she shot back, adjusting it slightly. "We consider hair
spiritual and private. A woman does not display her private parts."

Educated at the University of Michigan and Harvard Business School,
Rachel was immersed in her career until destiny took her by the hand and
led her to her husband, a yeshiva *bocker* (student). She has come a long
way. A baby boomer, she experienced the outrageous days of the hippie
generation. Now, however, she is in charge of a highly successful business, which she operates from offices on the second floor of her home.

I BELIEVE IN *destiny; you have a* beshert, *an intended. I met my husband when I got interested in Judaism, when I contacted the Rabbinical
College.*

My parents were not at all religious. Totally secular, very typical for American Jewish families. We had a menorah, we had matzoh on Passover, we visited Bubbah and Zaida. My mother, God bless her, sent me to an after-school program, mostly boys studying for bar mitzvah. I didn't believe in it, so I dropped out. How did I become religious? It happened while I was in Harvard. I didn't instantly become religious, mind you, but I began the journey.

It was destiny how I met my husband. He was a yeshiva student at the Rabbinical College. He went to Israel for the Yom Kippur War, a hippie kid, eighteen, long hair, the whole thing. Israel triggered his Jewish awareness, and when he came back he went directly to yeshiva. He came out five years later. He had no driver's license, no credit cards, no checkbook. When we got married he brought his wordly goods in two shopping bags. That was my husband. We don't have conflicts, but we do talk a lot about our spirituality.

I work constantly, every day. And then there's shabbat, two different things. My everyday week is probably a lot like everybody else's. Except we say the morning prayers, wash our hands, and then I come downstairs. The girls are home, the two boys are away in school. The difficult parts are the same as for any working mother. And the holidays are demanding, they require a lot of preparation. So I'm going crazy in September. It's very, very hard, it's a challenge to my mind, and I totally shut down my business on Yom Kippur. We don't answer the phone. And I think virtually all of my clients do respect what I'm doing.

I produce training programs for corporations; they spend millions of dollars on training. They're always coming out with new products and messages to communicate to people. It could be a ten- to twelve-minute video or an hour-long motivational kickoff for the entire sales force. I'm working on one now for Morgan Stanley Dean Witter.

My husband is also in a straight job — he works for a software development company. The Rabbinical College was a spiritual journey for him, not to become a rabbi, but as a foundation to be a Jew. It was oriented toward spriritual awakening, his duty, and the things we need to do in life.

I believe God gives us instructions, and a good Jew is supposed to fol-low them. It was God's will I have five children. We don't practice birth control, we practice family planning which, one of my teachers said, is planning a big family. So I had five boom-boom-boom.

You should have seen me ten years ago when there were five little ones. Now it's a piece of cake. I did have help, I'm not into being a martyr, but I work very hard.

In the early days I had complaints about my husband's parenting, many complaints, but in the last years he's getting better. Now that the boys are older he relates to them. But with the babies I nursed five kids and I didn't miss a day of work. I was very tired, we had financial prob-lems, marriage problems, I was ticked off with him all the time. We had our tough times. But we're stronger for it and we're better and something clicked.

I would say ten years minimum till the guys get the clue what it's all about. They're very immature, it doesn't really enter their brain. When you're a Lubavitch girl in classes you hear: "When a Lubavitch boy gets married, it's like moving into a well-run hotel. You will find, dears, that most of the complaints come from you."

Lubavitch women feel less tired as we get older, simply because we're not caring for babies anymore, not pregnant any more. You sort of wel-come menopause. You were tired, sick, your nipples hurt, the house was always messy. I'm getting out of that stage, and you forget the pain. A blessing God gives us. I'm told by grandparents that I'm going to be even more glad when the grandchildren come.

There's just a lot of self-sacrifice. A religious life is a life of sacrifice; there are times when it's tough and you feel you've denied yourself.

Kids cost money just to feed and clothe them. But on top of that, re-ligious families have private school tuition which is enormous. It's just like a mortgage, like college tuition. The boys, I think it runs about thirteen thousand each, and one is in Chicago, so bringing him home is expensive.

I don't think I would have had this business or the success that I have.

Like they say, "necessity is the mother of invention." I had to make money; it wasn't "I think I'll fulfill myself." I wanted to have the material goods. I made sacrifices to have my job. And my family has made sacrifices.

Like this morning. I'm always on the phone, and I wanted to get a proposal out. So I got up early, and I was still at the computer at seven-thirty when the girls got up. And Ruthie said, "Mommy, work didn't start yet." She's looking at her watch.

In other words, they insist on their time. And she's right, they're entitled to mommy, you know, for breakfast. And they get real, real upset after school when five-thirty, six-thirty rolls around and I'm still working.

When you have your own business, you work around the clock. And if there's a deadline, I'll give them dinner and go back to work. Entrepreneurs have no hours. I'm tired.

And yet miraculously kein ayin hora, *business comes. God sends you the business. So yes, I believe in miracles, things happen due to divine intervention, definitely. We don't know God's reasons. Godliness is hidden, and while we're in a state of exile—until the Messiah comes—we don't know how God works, we don't know why God does what He does. Lubavitchers don't claim to have any inside track, we don't know why we suffer, we don't know how many times we cycle here. We believe the Messiah's going to come and all souls will be eventually resurrected.*

It's funny. People make fun of us talking about the Messiah. But basically scientists are saying: "If we continue at this rate, the world cannot sustain itself." There's tremendous health issues, social issues, you got kids going into school shooting other children. People are afraid to walk on the streets.

You have to understand that for us the whole dating thing is a no-no. Parents have a big role, you have candidates that you present to the child. I have an eighteen year old. Parents put out feelers: What young men are available and looking? You ask around.

Weddings today are thirty, forty thousand dollars, I'm told. I'm working for the money. If I did not need the money, there's plenty I could do in the world with my talents. If I didn't have to work for money, I'd be working for Jewish organizations, yes, building museums, schools, I mean I'd volunteer. I have the skills.

God gave us this blueprint for the world, try to follow it as best you can. His divine thinking is better than mine. With Jewish mothers, the prototypical mother, is our guilt, wanting to give everything to the kids. And you can't be in two places. Are you going to compromise your children or your work? In the end I probably compromised a little of both at various times. On the other hand, if I had only pursued my career I wouldn't, God forbid, have this beautiful family.

It's a Jewish thing that people ought to be educated, be informed, and be active. A Torah concept. We come to this world to make it a godly place. We're chosen to be a light unto the nations. It's a Jew's nature to strive to be educated and make the world a better place.

Rachel's commitment to Judaism is seen from a Lubavitch perspective. Her entire day is informed by religious observances. But the balancing act she performs as businesswoman and mother of five is familiar territory to all female entrepreneurs who work out of their homes.

Although Rachel is deeply spiritual and committed to following God's laws, she is also caught up in the material world, driven to earn money for a thirty- to forty-thousand-dollar wedding. Like many entrepreneurs, she is tired and stressed out.

The last quarter of the twentieth century saw the number of female-owned businesses multiply nearly twenty times, from 402,200 to almost 8 million, with women-owned companies generating nearly $2.3 trillion a year in sales. Some women are making money. So Rachel's laments, "I work constantly, every day" and "I'm working for the money," are not merely Jewish complaints; they also resonate among non-Jewish women.

Add to Rachel's responsibilities as a Lubavitch wife and mother the demands of the Jewish holidays. She is "going crazy in September," and she lets us know that "a religious life is a lot of sacrifice." Yet she is firmly entrenched in a square job, and she works strictly to make money. Working women in America, Jewish and non-Jewish, know that scenario.

What sets Rachel apart is her firm belief that "God has given us a blueprint." She believes in miracles, fate, and destiny. She also feels that "It's a Jew's nature to strive to be educated and make the world a better place."

You will hear this refrain frequently.

Leah

LEAH, 32, strides toward me in a snappy navy suit. She wears a *kipah* on her thick graying red hair. She welcomes me with a smile. She is *Rabbi* Leah and principal of a Conservative Jewish day school with 350 students from preschool to fifth grade. She is also the mother of a two-year-old daughter and wife of a congregational rabbi in Westchester County, New York. They live one block from his synagogue.

"We're not just a dual-career *family*, we are dual-career *rabbis*," she jokes. "And this school," she gestures fondly as we walk down the hall to her office, "well, I actually graduated from this school. My class had thirty students."

Raised by parents who were not particularly observant, her life changed dramatically when she was in fifth grade in public school. On her parents' return from a United Jewish Appeal mission to Israel, they were so energized and so overwhelmed, they became kosher, observed shabbat, and joined a synagogue where her father prayed every morning. Finally, they yanked Leah out of public school.

"It was a very big deal because my mother believed passionately in public education, and the worst fights of their marriage were over this."

Ironically, Leah's evolving journey to becoming a rabbi began at Cornell, the school she chose because it was *not* particularly Jewish.

THAT'S WHERE I *found I really loved Judaism, at Cornell. I both loved it and rebelled against it, and I was terrified. I thought about a Ph.D., which I have now, but that was not the path I was seeing for myself. Women rabbis were a new thing, and I was very scared. I had no mentor. I didn't know a single woman rabbi. It was very new, and my parents were shocked. It took a long time of soul-searching before I could tell anybody.*

But at nineteen I decided to become a rabbi. I wasn't doing it to prove women could. It wasn't a statement about feminism or pioneering. It was what I wanted to do. To give to the world, to contribute. I was ordained at twenty-six. You are talking to someone whose whole life is led by Jewish patterns and traditions; [I'm] immersed in it.

We were married five years before our daughter was born. We put off having children because we were both working on a doctorate, both trying to put our careers into place.

Today, as principal of a Jewish day school, I see Jewish working women, divorced and married. Yes, I see them in really stressful situations. Is the Jewish community giving them enough support? No! Definitely not.

We're not welcoming, and it's hard to become part of synagogue life. We're not kind to each other and we haven't done a good job creating a community where people can call for help. Families are living far apart, and we haven't found a way to step in and respond to the real changes in sociology.

We also fail to measure up in providing for people's spiritual quests. Look at the number of Jews converting to Buddhism. Their reason for leaving Judaism is the synagogues weren't fulfilling their needs. [See Karen, page 133.] They found a snobbishness and a negativity. Jews aren't nice to each other. A large number of converts to Buddhism are Jews. And these are people who have an intense *interest in religion. We're not meeting their needs.*

Work issues are another area. I'm up before six, and I leave before seven. We are both rabbis, and when we have late-night meetings, it

*causes us anxiety even though we have a nanny. As rabbis, we don't com-
pete, no. We have been real partners in an incredible way. We could
never both be congregational rabbis, no, no, it would destroy us as a family. A congregational rabbi, well, it's all-consuming, and you need to live
walking distance from the synagogue. And the hours you put in are family time, so we are often there as a family. My husband is very happy with
what he does, and I'm very happy being Principal. I feel grateful, I have
talent for this, I contribute, I feel fulfilled.*

*But I see working women who are overburdened. And I'm lucky be-
cause I have a system in place that works for me. I leave work about four-
thirty, and when I'm home that time is for my daughter. I don't like to say
"quality time" because it implies that doing normal things are not quality. If I have to get to the supermarket, it becomes an outing, a game, we
do it together. She's a terrible sleeper so I have plenty of time with her to
nine-thirty. We have dinner together and spend the whole evening. I used
to call in every day, but not anymore. My husband works a block away,
so he ends up taking her to the pediatrician. I have the long commute.*

But yes, there are moments I feel overwhelmed.

*Last Friday I brought her to work and gave her a lot of toys and she
played on the floor in my office. I didn't have meetings, so I was able to
get a fair amount of work done. And today my husband took her to work
because our nanny was unavailable.*

*In February I was a speaker at the Hadassah convention in New
York. They're launching Hadassah Leadership Academy, a three-year
training program to develop women as leaders. I may participate. I'm
very organized.*

*The hardest part is, what do I do for me, for Leah? And that part just
falls out of the picture. The truth is by the end of the day, by the time
she's asleep, it's time to get things done for the next day. A half hour talking with my husband and I'm exhausted and go to sleep.*

*What I give up is time together with my husband. We don't go out so-
cially with other couples or even alone. There just isn't time, and if I hit
night meetings, well, that's it. Museums? Concerts? Forget about it, it's*

not happening. On my commute, I listen to books on tape. It's hard, I miss reading. And his job has social demands, so we spend a lot of time with his congregation. My closest friends are struggling with the same issues of work and family, and we understand if we don't return a phone call for a week.

My husband never could imagine marrying someone who didn't work. When I've said "Maybe I should stay home," he's said "Do whatever you want." But if I stayed home—it's been a fleeting thought but not a serious consideration—I'd miss all this.

Working women make assumptions about what a mother should be. But the role of women has changed dramatically. Judaism itself has followed *in terms of accommodating to egalitarian roles. Women became rabbis long after they participated in other professions.*

Judaism has seen women in the role of wife and mother and has praised that as a value. So changing that—well, talk about Jewish guilt! You know we can't get parents to come to a night meeting. Conflicts with work make it difficult. The stress level when a nurse has to call a working mother to pick up a sick child is intense. "How do I manage?" And volunteering here, well, they say "I can't be here, I work." [See Elinor, page 78.]

Jewish women are overly intense, *yes, oh yes, and that's probably how we function. Yes, there's an intensity among Jewish women. I deal with mothers, and their passion and commitment and anxiety is central and overwhelming. It is not uncommon for a working mother to burst into tears because she's trying to make everything work and that's not always possible. "Intense" is the word for it. We are intense about doing right for our children.*

On the weekends, I have great joy being with my daughter because I'm very conscious of time going by quickly, and these years don't come back. She's very precious to me, and being with her is the most rewarding time.

Do I ever feel guilty, for leaving her? Every day, every day. I always feel guilty, and I think how nice it would be to be a full-time mom. But I know I'd miss work. I have made a choice, and no choice is perfect. I still tell her, "I'm happiest when I'm with you, I love to be with you." And I make a big deal out of it when I have a day off.

I don't think it's rationalization. I want to be a working mom for her, a model. I want her to have options. She knows our routine, she's comfortable. I went back to work after six weeks, I nursed her until she was two. The day I bought formula was an incredible tension.

I'm lucky because my husband is very much a partner in our parenting, he's a very hands-on dad. But I do spend more time with her, I take on the bath, the teeth brushing, the stuff that has to get done. I do the food shopping, he does the cooking. But more of the housework and childcare falls on me. He will say "How can I help?" but it's always me who is doing the planning. The ultimate responsibility is mine.

I'd love to have a morning to sleep late.

I'd love to see a movie with my husband.

Leah's evaluation of our synagogues' failure to support women and the slow response to women seeking ordination as rabbis is disturbing. Orthodox women are still not permitted to be rabbis, and this is unacceptable to many feminists. Leah, however, describes her own spiritual journey to becoming a rabbi as a *non*feminist reaction: "I wasn't doing it to prove women could."

However, the long quest for women's equality came as a result of feminist politics. One Jewish woman was in the forefront. Betty Friedan's ground-breaking 1963 book, *The Feminine Mystique*, ignited women to use their potential as educated and talented people. Jewish and non-Jewish women were roused to action.

Indeed, Betty Friedan made Rabbi Leah possible. So did other Jewish feminists, including Gloria Steinem and Letty Cottin Pogrebin, co-founders of *Ms. Magazine*. Thanks in part to the efforts of these political activists, census figures show that a higher percentage of women than men complete high school and college. For the year 2000, census figures almost certainly will show that women account for more than half of the U.S. workforce.

Indeed, women rabbis no longer turn heads. Jewish women can even serve as *mohelim*, performing circumcisions and welcoming boys into the Jewish community.

Bernice

Like Leah, BERNICE, 56, is a rabbi. But she came to the rabbinate via a different route. Ordained in 1985 at age 43, she earned her master's in Hebrew letters. Her twenty-year marriage ended in a divorce and left her the single mother of two teenagers. Today she is the pulpit rabbi of a huge and handsome Reconstructionist synagogue in Pennsylvania.

We are seated in her private office. She is at her desk. I am facing her, the tape recorder between us. It is a large sunny room and she speaks so softly I have to lean in. She adjusts her rimless glasses and frowns as she seeks the right words. She wants to be precise. Her wakeful brown eyes are full of patience.

She explains that Reconstructionism has welcomed women rabbis since the mid-1960s and half of their rabbis are women.

What started her on her journey?

MY FATHER WAS *a Zionist; we were secular, but we had a strong Jewish identification and emotional ties to Israel.*

When my husband and two little girls, three and five, were living in Denver, we went to Israel to live for six years. Those years in Israel made me realize how much I loved Jewish life and rituals and traditions. It was the seventies and I began to think about being a rabbi.

My husband continued to be secular. He was not comfortable about the direction I was going in, and there were interpersonal problems too. He was a physician, into spiritual healing and psychic phenomena; and I was becoming more self-confident and self-assured, no longer a housewife and teacher. It created friction. So when we returned to live in Philadelphia because he had an offer—actually it was in my second year of rabbinical college — we divorced. I felt very guilty about our daughters, I certainly did; they were thirteen and fifteen, teenagers.

Maybe the hand of God was at work, because in Philadelphia there were Reconstructionists. I was very scared about becoming a rabbi, very unsure, and I was still reeling from the divorce. That was the worst period for us.

Then I met my second husband. He was divorced with four grown children and we just clicked. We were married in 1989 and there were no problems about blended families because our children were all grown. He is a psychiatrist — no psychic healing — quite mainstream. He writes prescriptions and listens.

Being a pulpit rabbi, I work every weekend and all day Sunday, nine to nine. Also many evenings I have meetings. He is very independent, no complaining about my hours, that I'm available all the time. In fact, I keep a kosher home — with Reconstructionists, it's a matter of individual choice. He is secular and calls this my mishigahs. It's my thing and he cooperates. He supports me totally and I support him going out for a bacon, lettuce, and tomato sandwich, sure.

Although I'm not raising small children, I still have to balance a family life, my husband, and his needs. And I have a grandchild and one on the way. I want to spend time with them. Theater? Concerts? No, no, we like to be at home. The weekends are taken up, but I structure time off during the week and we play on his day off.

The two best times of my life were when I was in Israel and when I was home with my children. I don't think that women rabbis can do this [pulpit] work with small children. Unless their husband is a househusband.

[Observing] women congregants, I see them running from one thing to another. Time. Time. They're trying to give their children time, their husband, their house. Husbands are helping out a lot. But working women with small children are pleasing the boss and the husband and the children, and they're just on go-go-go-go-go. They're torn apart, and my heart goes out to them. Do they get a chance to just sit down and be instead of doing?

Some women are very good, very good at balancing all these things. But mommy is getting shortchanged and she's missing out on a lot. Her profession is very important to her and she gets a lot of satisfaction from the status and being professionally competent.

We have 250 families here and most of the working women have their children in daycare and the children seem to be doing all right. I see mom and dad working as a team, but there's no one pattern. [Although] when the woman is more high-powered than the husband, he'll become a househusband.

If you're an observant family, being Jewish tells you to do shabbat and come to services, and that makes the choices easier. Families with small children fit this in in a positive way, and they tell me this is what enables them to keep their sanity. The synagogue is not an extra chore. They say that with all the stress, we've got to go to the synagogue. We need our spiritual nourishment, we need our sanity injection.

For some women, the holidays are a stress and they look at it like it's a burden. They experience it as a burden, not an opportunity to bring something meaningful into their home. Which may be a reflection of the secularization of American Judaism. We're becoming more and more distant from the meaning of tradition, and Judaism is less and less part of our lives. On Passover, they say "I'll be glad when the holidays are over."

We are not only a religion, we are a civilization. There is more than just the sense of being a Jewish family and weaving it into our lives. But parents are pulled in so many different directions.

A Christian woman can compartmentalize and go to church on Sunday and feel she's done it. But for Jewish women, there are things we have to do in the home as a family. Ideally, it's part of our lives, it's all interwoven. Judaism is a civilization. We have a language, a culture, traditions, and rituals.

There's a tremendous Jewish population in America that is making a conscious effort to incorporate Judaism into their lives. Among the generation coming up, in their thirties and forties, they are more spiritual, seeking spirituality.

Until now, 50 percent of us could not express ourselves religiously. But now Jewish women can take a more active participation in our religion. This has produced a tension between Orthodox and feminists and it's caused conflict. But it has enriched Judaism tremendously.

Bernice's experiences as a "pulpit" rabbi corroborate Leah's experiences of her husband's work as a "congregational" rabbi. The job of heading a synagogue is all-consuming. Does that militate against women rabbis? Certainly not. Perhaps age is an important factor. Young female rabbis—Leah is thirty-two, a generation removed from Bernice's fifty-six—enjoy the partnership of a husband in childraising. Such partnerships, uncommon twenty years ago, will become normative in the twenty-first century.

As Jewish working women become wealthier and better educated, it is unlikely that they will return to being stay-at-home moms. And husbands like and need their wives' paychecks. One doesn't have to be a feminist to see the handwriting on the wall: Jewish working women will form even closer bonds with their husbands as financial partners for the family's well-being.

In their book *Gender Equality and American Jews*, Moshe and Harriet Hartman note that "the tendency to gender equality in secular attainment is a Jewish pattern" and "tendencies toward gender equality seem to be rooted in Jewish patterns of behavior." Conclusion? Jews encourage equality between husband and wife, at least in theory.

However, Bernice, observing 250 families from her Reconstructionist pulpit, notes young Jewish mothers on the "go-go-go-go-go." Jewish fathers are just not beset by the same level of pressure. Bernice also suggests that the multiple pressures experienced by Jewish working women may cause a decline in their allegiance to Judaism. They are just too busy and too tired to keep up even nominal observances.

Indeed, *The Jewish Environmental Scan toward the Year 2000*, published by the Council of Jewish Federations in 1992, reaches similar conclusions. It states that the core Jewish population will start to decline after the year 2000 and that American Jews will continue to be predominantly secularized. Whether the thirty and forty year olds Bernice sees as "seeking spirituality" can reverse this trend remains to be seen.

Finally, Bernice is right on target when she notes that many women experience the holidays as a burden. I am writing this one week before Passover and I have just come from the Jewish Community Center gym where the topic on everyone's mind is the upcoming seder. Jewish working women, grappling with preparations, are in Passover Anxiety! What to serve? Where to buy? Supermarkets offer aisles of kosher foods, and a kosher version of almost anything is available — balsamic vinegar to sushi, ketchup, Oreos, and even peach sorbet. But we still find things to worry about: I overheard a debate over kosher-for-Passover paper towels and kitchen faucet covers. Yet another way of making us crazy.

Aya

Like Rachel, Leah and Bernice, AYA, 29, is a deeply religious woman. She is also a psychologist completing her Ph.D., and the mother of a son, 2.

Born in the United States, she was taken to Israel at age one when her parents, Zionist and *not* religious, made *aliya*. For six years, they lived on Moshav Shitufi, a socialistic mix between moshav and kibbutz.

"When we returned to live in Florida, I was seven. And in the airport, I *vowed* to myself that I will go back! It's significant to me, this dream to return to Israel."

In Florida, as a teenager devoted to the *Rocky Horror Picture Show*, she had her first Orthodox experience at a Young Judea summer camp. "It was the eighties and my whole life revolved around my own personal love for Israel." But she couldn't imagine herself being Orthodox. Brought up by a feminist mother who always worked and believed in the empowerment of women, the Orthodox life presented a conflict.

A tall, slender young woman with a shiny auburn bob and fierce hazel eyes, Aya remembers how she felt. "I didn't know where to go with that." Then her eyes light up. "Until I went back to Israel for a year after high school."

It was 1987, and with her best friend she traveled all over the country. "And we realized, we were keeping kosher and keeping the sabbath."

She pauses and grins. "I also met my husband. He was *shomar shabbat*, observant of the sabbath. He was in uniform, wearing a *kipah*. And to me that was perfect."

It happened at a significant point in her life. Indeed, Aya and her husband come from similar backgrounds. He was born in Boston and his parents, like hers, made aliya.

HE WAS TWENTY-ONE, *[doing] four years in the army. I called my parents and told them I wasn't coming home. And I joined the army. They hung up. A very stressful time. But I served in the Israeli army three years and I married him at age twenty-two. It was understood that my choice was to live in Israel. It was my dream since age seven. And joining the army was my way to go into Israeli society. The first year of our marriage we lived on a moshav with his family.*

After the army, I went to Bar-Ilan in Ramat Gan for my B.S. in psychology. At that point, we both decided I should apply in the States for a Ph.D. He had his B.S. in computer programming and we agreed as long as it was minimal time, maybe two years, and temporary. I was pregnant with my son and he supported me 100 percent in this. He was open to change.

Today, I'm at the Miami Institute of Psychology and right now my husband is the sole breadwinner. Our intention is to return to Israel as soon as I get my Ph.D. I'm a full-time student and he sees this as something we're doing together. He's paying, but it's our money and my future and his future. And we're very together on this. We had times when he was in the army and he was the student, and I was earning the money. So he understands that we are investing in my future, which is our future.

Raising our son, that's the hard part. We both decided our priority is our son and future children — breastfeeding, the whole deal. No daycare for three years. We would be with him. We follow the philosophy of "attachment parenting." It's a specific parenting style that encourages mothers to be full-time mothers and fathers to support mothers during this initial period. And the women to be proud of their roles as mothers, that it's not a belittling thing. I used to think my life would be I'd have a great job and my children would kind of fit in around my career. [Now], I wouldn't turn my child over to a nanny, or an au pair, or a housekeeper. Women who do that are fooling themselves. They say it's fine because if they thought otherwise they couldn't be happy. They're justifying their experience. They're making a big mistake. They're blind to their children's problems or it'll show up later when they're twenty [and say] "Mom wasn't there for me." You can't go back, it's done.

I think our [parenting style] has a cost, yes. But the cost would have been if I had chosen not to put the effort into my son. I think as a woman my development is as a mother, too. I feel very lucky that I can develop in both areas, my career and motherhood, without feeling compromised. The first three years are so critical, the impact on the child. As a psychologist, I do know the impact can show up years later in different ways.

For my profession, I'm not sure what role I'll play in Israel — how they'll accept me or where I'll work, because of my role as a parent. I'll pick a place to work where I can choose my hours and have babies and be away for six months and go back very slowly and part time. I don't plan to work full time until they're beyond three. And it could be ten years, because I plan to have more children. My husband and I agree on this. But I'm not suggesting women shouldn't work.

The way we have worked it out is I go to school at night, my husband comes home early from work, and we have timeframes when each one is responsible. We live with my parents. It's temporary, and it works out because we have grandparents and uncles and other people for periods of a couple of hours. And a cleaning woman, but she's not responsible for [our child's] discipline or education in any way; she's a babysitter.

We haven't had a vacation because we enjoy his company so much we don't feel we need to get away. We have treasured times alone, when he's asleep or we go out on a date. In Israel we live in an Orthodox community and we socialize all the time. Here it's a family thing; if we go out to dinner, my mom babysits. We have another year and a half in America and then back to Israel!

I want to make it clear that I'm lucky to experience a professional identity now. And I think it's important for a woman to get that experience beforehand, but not to expect to develop 100 percent in her profession while her children are growing up. I have that identification as a psychologist and I can go right into it when I feel the need. It's important for a woman to have a role outside the home. But the children and the family should be the priority always, not just the first three years.

Feminism has impacted on me and all my peers, yes. We're all dealing with it and trying to define it for us. It was a pendulum and went to extremes, the voices were strident, and the role of the mother was lost. Women have to be vocal and corporations have to change. But we should not belittle our role as a woman.

The trade-off might be I'm not going to become a renowned psychologist. Or I won't be earning $130,000 a year. No great cars and less money. But we have our priorities straight. I look at the way I feel and I feel very happy, very secure. Very fulfilled and blessed. I look at my child and I can see how confident he is. And I wonder how it could be better than that. Of course I believe it was beshert that I got here.

What I say about parenting is what I found in my psychology work. What I find Judaically are the lessons I learn as I grow spiritually. And they confirm what I know about the role of the mother in Judaism.

It's not to say I don't have my conflicts with Orthodox Judaism. I don't wear long skirts and I don't cover my hair and I swim in a pool with men and women and I feel comfortable wearing a bathing suit. There are a lot of contradictions. This is modern Orthodox Judaism, as opposed to Lubavitch or Hassidic or Satmar. It's fair to say I'm a modern Orthodox woman engaged in the commercial world, yet attached to the spiritual world.

I'd like to make changes in the orthodox community. Like women not

*being able to get their get [a religious divorce] unless the husband agrees.
And I would support women counted in the minyan. I think there's movement toward these changes.*

*With work and family, it's a real balancing act and I wouldn't be able
to do it without my husband. He's with me 100 percent.*

What can we say about affiliated, deeply committed American Jews
like Rachel, Leah, Bernice and Aya? The numbers are tricky when we
identify Jews by denomination.

Researchers at the Jewish Theological Seminary provided figures
from *The North American Survey of 1995–1996.* Only about *half* of
those who claimed to be Conservative, for example, were actually
members of a synagogue. The data showed that synagogue membership in the United States breaks down to Orthodox 11 percent, Conservative 47 percent, and Reform 36 pecent. Add it up and you get 94 percent. Presumably, the other 6 percent is accounted for by very small
numbers of Lubavitch, Hassidim, Satmars, Reconstructionists, and secular Jews.

We get different figures from a 1990 survey by *Jewish Communities of
the World:* Orthodox 6 percent, Conservative 35 percent, and Reform
38 percent. These findings indicate that half of American Jews are affiliated with a synagogue, but only a third attend regularly.

Let's leave those numbers. I prefer to rely on the individual voices of
Jewish women. Here you have heard four deeply spiritual working
women grappling with the problems of the contemporary world.

In the next chapter, you will meet two women for whom religious
values take a backseat to work. They put in long hours and travel time
as part of a deep commitment to their jobs. I call them *workaholics.*

Are they conflicted? Do they feel guilty?

While the religious women in this chapter are guided by "God's
voice," these workaholics are governed by secular values. Lest we rush
to judge their priorities, let's listen to their side.

2

WORKAHOLICS

ERICA

BETH

Picture a workaholic and who do you think of? A man. He puts in a twelve- to fourteen-hour day and comes home exhausted. His wife, probably working outside the home, has taken care of the children, done the food shopping and laundry, cooked the meals, helped the kids with their homework, gone to a school meeting, made weekend plans, and done all the other tasks that go with running a home and a family.

At eight or nine when the workaholic arrives home, his wife turns her attention to him. Serves him dinner, asks about his day, tells him about the children, who called, what mail came in, and whatever family business needs attention. He's a decent dad, so he plays with his kids if they're still awake. Maybe he has more work to do at home, papers to go over, preparations for the next day. Around eleven or twelve, he falls into bed.

What's the payoff for this workaholic's life?

For many men, it's the sense of achievement for a job well done. If he's also bringing in a large income, the payoff is the money he earns and the advantages it confers. Family vacations. Fancy cars. Private schools and summer camps. The family understands that daddy works very hard to provide them with the best in life. Remember the hard-working Mr. Patimkin in Philip Roth's *Goodbye Columbus?*

For Jewish families, the role of "good provider" is part of what my mother used to call a "good catch." While Jewish girls were not encouraged to marry for money, many understood that falling in love with a rich man made life a lot more pleasant. It followed, therefore, that wives should understand their "good provider" husbands and be grateful to them. A workaholic husband was excused from domestic duty, forgiven lapses in sexual attention, and, in some families, even coddled.

Now switch genders. Make the workaholic a *woman.*

She is a wife and a mother and a contender in the workplace. How can she do it all? What does it cost her? Do her children suffer? Is her marriage headed for the rocks? Is she selfish and ego-driven? Or does she simply love her job? What impels her to be a workaholic?

Women workaholics, married and single, Jewish and Gentile, are a growing breed. In this chapter you'll meet two Jewish women who challenge many of the ideas we hold about the sanctity of family life.

Erica

ERICA, 40, is not your ordinary working mom. She earns well over half a million dollars a year as a senior partner in an international consulting firm. She travels extensively worldwide.

On this dark, bone-chilling night, as I wait to interview her, she pulls into her long circular driveway close to 8:30 P.M. She has made three calls from her cell phone to tell her husband she's running late, traffic is heavy, and she's sorry to keep me waiting. Their daughter, 7, and son, 9, are in the den, watching television and eating off snack tables. She wears a smart navy suit and discreet gold earrings, nothing showy. She is small and slim. Her dark hair is fashionably cropped, and her face is thin and sharp and intelligent.

Within minutes of her arrival, her husband serves her dinner on the dining-room table and disappears as we talk over the meal he's prepared. First, a tall glass of water and a green salad, then a small portion of pasta and a slice of Italian bread.

Her voice is soft and controlled. Eating, she never loses her focus. She is confident and firm in her answers, no waffling, no hesitations.

Between bites, she tells me that she was raised in a Reform home, though her mother kept kosher. She attended Hebrew school during high school and was confirmed. She went to the University of Pennsylvania, which she describes as "having a large number of Jewish students." She earned an M.B.A. at Wharton.

AT WHARTON *I decided product management was what I wanted to do. I was very goal oriented and I loved math. I thought it would be more practical to earn an M.B.A. I began work with General Foods Corporation in the marketing area. They were one of the premier consumer packaging companies and I stayed five years.*

In 1986 I joined Fostergold International [not the real name]. I'm there twelve years. It's an international general management consulting firm. We serve typically large corporations on strategy, operations, and organization. I am a director. There are 220 directors. We have 4,000 consultants worldwide.

I'm making well over five hundred thousand dollars a year and I fly all over the world. This year, I probably flew 120 segments on one airline alone. Internationally, I was in London two or three times, Scandinavia twice. I travel around the United States two or three times a week, constantly. A lot of day trips. I have clients in Washington, [in] Texas. It's a very long day. Physically exhausting, but you get used to it.

I get on a plane the way some people get on a bus, to me it's not that big a deal. I arrive just before takeoff, I fly first class, I stay in nice hotels. Brazil and Argentina I do in two days. I also spend a lot of time in Tel Aviv; I have a client there so I went three or four times last year. If the flight leaves at ten or eleven at night, it's a glass of water, a pillow, and I go to sleep. If I go to Copenhagen, I take an overnight flight and I sleep. When I arrive, I take a shower and work all day. You don't let it stop you.

Why do I work so hard? There are so many satisfactions.

Intellectually, it is very challenging and exciting. I work with CEOs of multibillion-dollar companies. Fortune 50 companies. We work on some of the most challenging issues that exist. I do a lot of work in the consumer area, in retailing, in building systems that improve the entire merchandising flow process. How you buy goods, how you distribute them to multiple locations, how to grow businesses. Plus merger work. I find that so interesting. We develop relationships, and negotiation is part of what we do. Our firm is very much into research on issues relevant to our client—a lot of problem solving. It's a lot of fun.

It's also people-intensive, so there's a lot of interesting interactions with client executives to help them be successful. There's a lot of stress involved, sure, we're only as good as the work we do. So you are forever testing your ability. We consider ourselves the most eminent in the world.

Let's go back to satisfactions. We have a meritocracy, so we are reviewed every year and elected to levels based on our client impact. I've gotten to the senior level in the firm, that's a satisfaction. I have governing responsibilities now within the firm itself; that requires me to work with offices outside the United States. For example, I'm evaluating people in Scandinavia and Eastern Europe. And my clients move around. That comes with senior partnership.

My husband agreed with my decison, we knew there was travel. In fact, on the first assignment I was gone four days a week for six months. That was before we had kids. It was manageable.

Do I ever feel guilty about being away? Yes, but this is what I do! It comes with the territory. Sometimes the kids get frustrated if I'm traveling, but I try very hard to get to the soccer game and I know in advance when the winter concert is. During the week, I see them a little bit in the morning and when I get home at night.

Tonight is a typical night. The kids go to bed nine, nine-thirty. I have only an hour with them. I'm up at five-forty, six-thirty, and putting in a fourteen-hour day is not news. So what's left over for the kids? Well, it's not all fourteen hours of stress. And on the weekends I spend as much time as I can with them. Every chance I get. I believe in quality time.

With my first, my son, I took four or five months off and I went back part time for a while. I have a housekeeper who lives in and she takes care of the children and the house. With the second, a daughter, I took six months off and then went back full time. The kids don't complain. My husband will attend a school meeting if I can't.

The hardest part of the balancing act is to do everything I'd like to do. Like help them with their homework. There are things you want to do, but you can't. Like reading in bed. And I'd like to work out. Spend time with friends. My closest friends are professional women—doctors, lawyers, businesswomen. We tend to see each other various times a year, over a weekend.

Last year I decided to learn Hebrew because my oldest was ready to start Hebrew school and I did a Haftorah portion [the weekly reading, not part of the Pentateuch] . Our temple stresses that a family has to be involved. So when my kids go on Sundays, I go with them and I take lessons.

Am I missing the most precious moments? Am I fooling myself?

I think my children have experiences other children don't have. They are growing up in a household where our roles and lives reflect everything men and women can achieve. I want them to see that. We travel, and in our economic status my children have access to things other children don't have. It's important to me that they travel and see the world. I feel very strongly that, because I travel, my children should see what this is.

Ultimately, if I didn't like what I did, it wouldn't be worth the travel. If you're happy, your kids get a lot more out of you.

My mother thinks I travel too much, and I'm trying to cut back—it's not that enjoyable. The balancing act . . . well, if you like what you do and accomplish what you want, a lot of things happen.

In my fourteen-hour workday, my kids are surrounded by a lot of peo-

ple who are very good to them. We live close to my family, and my mother, particularly since her retirement, spends time with them; she's here. She gives them each one activity after school, and she works on homework with them a couple of times a week. And she's always there as a backup. And my husband works close by. If my kids get sick and I'm not here, someone else will do it. They accept it. That's all they know.

I can keep this up several more years; I don't want to do it forever. But I'm the kind of person now who would not be satisfied working in a corporate environment. I'm capable of doing this and I should have the opportunity. This is what I studied for, this is what I worked for. I decide the clients I serve, what I do, where I go. Every day is different. It's very diverse, very interesting. I can have a huge impact on my clients.

Sounds like it's all about me? My achievements and what I'm entitled to? My children? They're entitled to a great life. My family is the most important thing in my life. If they needed me to, I would walk away from this. But! I've found a way to do both. If I can't, I won't. I think my kids are very well adjusted. They do very well in school, they're smart, they have friends, they're considerate, and they're good people. That impresses me. So I look at that and say "They're just fine." I don't see that this is so complicated or so different.

What do I have that other women don't have? Well . . . you need to be highly motivated. Very well organized and disciplined. And you need a very good support system.

At work, I have a great secretary I rely on, that's all part of it. At home, we're very lucky with our housekeeper. If my kids didn't like who was here, it wouldn't work. At this point in our life, they're in school. They went to pre-school young, when they were two, so they've been influenced by a lot of people. I'm proud of the relationship we have with them.

This juggling act, I couldn't do it if my husband weren't fully involved with the kids. He's comfortable with giving them showers and putting them to bed. It wouldn't work if he weren't, and he doesn't resent that I make a lot more than he does.

I think women in general should have more confidence in their ability. I come across a lot of women who simply project that it can't be done.

For Jewish women, the bind is they want to achieve, but they want to be the best parents possible. My parents sacrificed a lot, there was a great emphasis on education. They believed if you went to a great institution and studied with great people, in that kind of environment you're going to have opportunities and access others don't have. I graduated summa. For women this was our chance. It's a very complicated issue, very frustrating.

Having it all? I don't know what that means. But at this moment in time, it's okay, it's okay.

Five years from now, it could be different.

Although Erica's fourteen-hour work day and high earning power separate her from ordinary Jewish working moms, her educational and occupational achievements do mirror the fact that Jewish women far surpass other women and even the majority of American men in these areas.

In fact, few American men reach Erica's salary level and lifestyle. Male breadwinners who reach her level of attainment usually have a devoted wife running their home. Having interviewed hundreds of corporate wives for my book *Playing For High Stakes*, I met many wives of workaholics. These men traveled widely, were emotionally unavailable, and expected their stay-at-home wives to raise the kids.

In Erica's story, we see the reverse. Women workaholics face the problem of finding backup at home. They need housekeepers or husbands or mothers who take charge of their homes and their children.

By the 1980s, as women left home to go to work, the workplace deeply impacted family life. Arlie Hochschild's 1989 book *The Second Shift* explains how mothers joining the workforce brought about a revolution in the home. She looked at the division of domestic tasks, how working women dealt with feelings of guilt, and the huge gap between their stressful lives and their ideas. This forced women into impossible choices. Hochschild's later book, *The Time Bend* (1997), shows us how the boundary between work and home becomes unclear. Often the workplace becomes a surrogate home and the home becomes a workplace.

Erica, however, feels her life is under control. "I graduated summa. . . . I'm capable of doing this and I should have the opportunity." Are her kids in trouble? "I do what I do. I believe in quality time." Erica believes her children are "very well adjusted, smart, considerate, and good people."

Clearly, Erica could not do her demanding work, the travel time, and the fourteen-hour days without the support system she has put into place. Consider her backup. Her *mother* comes after school to help with the homework. A full-time, live-in *housekeeper*. A *husband* fully involved with the kids. "If my kids get sick . . . someone else will do it. . . . That's all they know."

Erica has important personal qualities: lots of energy, self-discipline, and good organizational skills. But equally important, her earning power pays for a housekeeper for her children. Her family is nearby to pitch in. Yet even Erica experiences the contradiction at the heart of Jewish working women, two tugs that pull them apart: "They want to achieve but they want to be the best parents possible." And she rejects the message other women accept, "that it can't be done." Then she makes it happen.

Women's attitudes changed dramatically in the 1970s. By the 1980s, working women who left the home for jobs transformed their families, making adjustments and compromises *because work became important*. By the 1990s, work was the driving force. Magazines like *Working Woman* and *Working Mother* flourished as women earning a paycheck felt the power, the independence, and the self-esteem their jobs conferred. It felt so good they were not willing to give it up.

The difficulty, of course, is that family responsibilities did not diminish.

Beth

BETH, 40, welcomes me into her Upper West Side apartment. It's Sunday morning and her husband is taking the children, 7 and 4, out for a walk. We talk in her living room, four floors above Manhattan's screeching sirens.

She is a tall, pretty woman with porcelain skin, short dark hair, and a gentle manner. She's thoughtful and cerebral. She is the product of a mixed marriage—her father is Jewish, her mother is a lapsed Catholic. Beth's husband is not Jewish.

"We celebrate Hanukkah and Christmas and Passover and Easter. Our celebrations are more cultural than religious. We don't go to synagogue or church."

It's December and she gestures to the menorah and Christmas cards on the mantle of the fireplace. Beth perceives herself as Jewish. "My father was comfortable with Judaism and my Jewish grandparents were around."

Beth works a full day at a prestigious university press, then lugs home manuscripts and puts in long evenings at her desk. Her husband has a master's in architecture, but switched to free-lance work to be Mr. Mom and work from home. It is her career that appears to come first.

AS EDITOR-IN-CHIEF *of a university press, my work is managing the editorial department and doing tasks such as budgeting, dealing with the board of trustees and faculty publications. I also acquire books on history and political science for my own lists. About twenty-five books a year, a big list.*

On an average workday, my husband and I alternate dropping our children off at school. At work, I deal first with all the electronic correspondence. I'd like to spend the morning doing editorial work and corresponding with authors, but by ten o'clock that's out the window be-

cause someone has a problem, a department issue, or a meeting. So what happens is I have to bring my editorial work home.

I do all that work at night when the children are asleep because I can never get to it during the day. I try to leave the office by six, but it's not a nine-to-five job, too much work. Publishing is an understaffed profession. I have fourteen people on staff and some days I feel as if my whole job is people issues. I wish I could get to the editorial work, but you can't just close the door to think about a manuscript. People keep coming in, so I end up bringing work home. Things that need [me to] focus, I take home.

Before I had a family, I'd stay late, but that had to stop. The kids go to bed eight-thirty, nine. Then I make their lunches and straighten up the apartment. Honestly, you're talking to someone who hasn't worked it out. I start working again by nine-thirty, ten, and if there's a crisis and I have to get something done, I dump the whole evening on my husband and say, "This is it, I'm going to work!" It depends how long I can stay up. I'm working all the time. It's a constant in publishing to bring the work home. What's missing is leisure, it's completely gone. That's the choice I had to make.

Actually I'm very lucky I can leave by six; not many jobs where you have a lot of responsibility and that much freedom. The former director had five children and a wife in the suburbs who magically raised them. But the new director has a working wife and he understands balancing a family and a job. He says, "Do whatever you want." As long as I do my work.

My husband is a free-lance graphic designer, actually an architect who grew to dislike it. He quit when our first child was born, and he stayed home to take care of her. A very unusual situation. We had no babysitter or daycare. For almost a year and a half, he was home. Then he started part time and she went to daycare. During that very hard time, I was working full time. But I had a huge advantage because I was leaving her only with her parent or my parents, who live close by and helped us out. Only recently did he start working full time.

My husband was very happy, he had no conflict, he wanted to be home with her. But he took a lot of questioning from his mother and brothers. He took a lot of flak and he had to defend himself. People thought he was throwing away his career and making a huge sacrifice.

I always knew he wanted to play a very large role in raising our child. And I always wanted to keep doing my work. But I didn't know he'd quit his job and do it full time, and I never expected it. I felt guilty and I did worry about him making the sacrifice, if his career would be okay. But I felt so good going to the office because she was with him. When I got home, she was bathed and he had [brought] some food in. No, dinner wasn't ready, but I knew she was cared for. There was still tons of work and we were up and down all night with her; she was colicky.

How did I get through it? I just remember being tired all the time, but wanting to do everything. And there was nothing I could stop doing because I wanted more than anything to have a family and to keep doing my work. What goes is getting any rest. No social life, no leisure. Someone on the board asked me, what did I do for hobbies? And I just laughed. He had no clue.

So I was the breadwinner. And we managed because my parents babysat, and they helped us out enormously. They were wonderful, they'd buy a snowsuit, a huge expense, and make it seem like they weren't helping us. And other essentials, the stroller. Those years we didn't do anything, maybe go out to dinner. We didn't want to leave her. She's seven now and our son is four and once, only once, we went for an overnight.

When my husband went back to work, we put her in a good daycare center. It's around eight thousand dollars a year for full time. And when our son was born we got a babysitter. We're always juggling.

Two years ago, my husband left part time to do freelance. He works out of the apartment, which means he's back to being my security at work. If someone's sick, he'll be the one to stay home. With my job it's very hard to cancel a meeting. I don't know how I could do this without a husband who's a support. I guess I have a wife. He's making the sacrifices careerwise. When the crunch comes, we just work it out case by case. And sometimes we call my parents and say, "Look, we need you for a few hours, I've got to get on the computer." There's a lot of just staying up late, a lot of late nights. We just don't get enough sleep.

The children turn to him. *A lot. Once our daughter fell at school and started crying, "I want my daddy, I want my daddy!" and it was the topic of discussion at the daycare center. The joke is three people are writing their thesis on it. Do I have any guilt? No. They have such a great relationship, I think this is so healthy. Two parents who are equally attached.*

Lots of people bring up the question of guilt and I feel strange saying "No, I don't feel guilty." I want my children to think I love them *and I love my* work. *It may not be a traditional arrangement, but it seems to be helpful to the children. So the answer is no, I don't feel guilty. In a way, I'd feel more guilty if my child felt I made a huge sacrifice and I was regretting my whole life.*

Of course there are moments. Like when my daughter says, "Valerie's mom picks her up at school every day, why can't you?" So I picked her up and took her to the office one day, and she loved it. It's a constant working out. I'm lucky to have work that's enriching and challenging. Yes, it's tiring. It's part of the way I am, what makes me feel excited and satisfied as a person. I'm a better parent because of that. No home-baked cookies. But if you have to choose, a happy mom is the better choice.

I'm not saying there aren't women who are perfectly happy staying home. But I do see a number of mothers who are not really happy, they're frustrated, they snap at their kids. Quality time? That's a myth. You can't come home, throw off your clothes, and sit on the rug with your kids. That's ridiculous, children don't work like that, they're not little robots. I have incredible discussions with my son when he's falling asleep, that's when he wants to talk.

In the end, children come first. It's a constant battle. A certain letter I wanted to write beautifully will go out because my son wanted to play dinosaurs. That's hard to accept, that you have to compromise. But the question is, does anyone notice our high standards? My level of being prepared for a meeting, my charts, and my organization? I feel terrible unprepared, but they're not perceiving it.

We demand a lot of ourselves. And we got to those positions because we worked incredibly hard. We have discipline, we're well organized, and every second of the day has to be productive. It makes us unbelievably efficient. It's a survival tactic.

But at home, lots of things go. Housework is marginally done and lunches get thrown together. For Halloween, pul-eeze! You call 1–800-SPIDERMAN for the costume, kids don't care. They want you to heat up chicken nuggets—they only eat three things in the whole world. Having you available emotionally is what counts. And your values.

It's interesting that we're talking around the holidays—it's gross, the materialism in our culture. I feel very strongly I need to reject that materialism and make it clear to our children the values that are important.

Our daughter goes to public school now. It was a conscious choice because I want her to grow up with children of different backgrounds. We don't have lots of money and I don't like certain groups and their values. I don't think forbidding things for political or intellectual reasons always works with kids, like, no Barbie because it teaches sexism, blah, blah. But we say, "You don't need a leather skirt, there are other choices." And my son is a very gentle child, and yes, he got a Spidersomething for Hanukkah. He's into superheroes; it's a thing boys work out.

A lot of women pretend nothing has to go, you can have it all, even with children. That's not true. Everything has to change. If "all" is having work you love and time with your family and cutting out lots of other things, that's having it all. But if [you're] working to midnight and going out on weekends with friends and traveling, you ignore your children. I do travel, yes, I go to publishing conferences and academic meetings. Short two- or three-day meetings every month, but no long trips. I take a 5 A.M. flight to get to a meeting in Chicago and [return] to be home at night.

Feminism has influenced me tremendously. In the sixties and seventies, I read everyone: Simone de Beauvoir, Betty Friedan, Gloria Stei-

nem, and I took women's studies in college. My whole life is a "feminist" lifestyle. But also I take a lot from traditional feminine roles. I worry if my children take their medicine. Because my husband has done so much raising the children, the last thing we fight about is who does the ironing. Our life is built around this partnership of letting me continue my work. I do "feminine" things—sewing, cleaning—he puts up bookcases. We don't fight about those things. Of course, my husband is a feminist! We have a true partnership. He was the one who moved to New York because my career was here. Feminism is part of the fabric of our lives.

Judaism calls for a much more traditional role for the mother than working women can have. Right there you've got an insurmountable conflict. It's very hard with a demanding job. And there's guilt and stress and this heightens the conflict. The guilt makes it harder.

Also, Jewish culture assumes that no matter how good the school is, the mother still [helps with] the homework and does the extra meetings and this produces stress. In other cultures, there is less supplementing education and constantly overseeing the reading and educational stuff. It comes out of the tremendous stress on education in Jewish households.

Many of us don't *want* to like these women workaholics, it goes against the grain. But we have to admit that some of the things they say make sense.

Erica and Beth, both forty, are enjoying challenging and satisfying work. They truly *love* their jobs, love the responsibilities and the decision making. Sure, they're exhausted, but so are most working women employed in far less appealing jobs. According to *Newsweek*, the National Sleep Foundation's 1998 poll found that 74 percent of women sleep less than eight hours per night, 16 percent sleep less than six hours per night, and most women employed don't get the rest they need. We are living in a sleep-deprived society where stressed-out working women are the norm, not the exception.

The issue is whether the children of workaholic mothers suffer. Some women workaholics may be irresponsible parents, but Erica and Beth work hard to carve out time with their children, who appear to be thriving. And there is growing evidence that with e-mail, faxes, cell phones, and beepers working mothers are keeping a close watch on their kids. And these two workaholic moms have provided capable and loving surrogates to do the parenting. Does it have to be the mother exclusively?

The assumption persists in our culture that *only* mothers can do it right. That fathers are meant to bring home the brisket and mothers are meant to cook it. Both Jewish and American cultures frown on workaholic mothers who seem to have made a bad choice, and ask us to assume that their children will be damaged. The message is that these women *should* feel guilty.

Therefore, when we see workaholic families thriving, we may well react suspiciously. The reversal of mother-father roles might be even harder to handle. When Beth's child called for "daddy" rather than "mommy," it became the talk of the daycare center. How many men really want to be "Mr. Mom"?

For Erica and Beth, working hard seems to be working. Their children are fine, their jobs are rewarding, their families are supportive. And they appear to be guiltless.

"Do I have any guilt? No," Beth tells us. "I think this is so healthy . . . two parents who are equally attached . . . I guess I have a wife," she admits; "he's making the sacrifice careerwise." In a crunch, both Erica and Beth count on grandma.

Erica says joyfully, "I found a way to do both!" Presumably to balance work and love.

Beth says confidently, "No home-baked cookies, but if you have to choose, a happy mom is the better choice."

Which is exactly what a plethora of books are now saying: guilt-ridden mothers do *not* make good parents. Indeed, Betty Holcomb's book *Not Guilty: The Good News about Working Mothers* and Rosalind Barnett and Caryl Rivers's book *She Works, He Works* tout the benefits of two-income families who are purported to be happier than single-income families. And Joan Peters's book *When Mothers Work* tells us that we can love our children without sacrificing ourselves.

Susan Chira, author of *A Mother's Place*, believes that "Mothers should be given the freedom to make choices without being . . . hounded by . . . the confining ideal of the perfect mother." Like Erica, Chira travels widely and guiltlessly, and her choice is supported by her husband.

If you read popular women's magazines, then I suspect you're seeing a turnaround on the guilt issue. *Working Mother* points out that twenty years ago mothers felt so guilty about going to work they had a regular column in the magazine called "The Guilt Department." Even ministers were denouncing the working mother. In 1990, the magazine found a changed culture. Most moms said they felt only occasional pangs of guilt. My guess is that these young mothers were raised to have a career, and work is part of the fabric of their lives.

Erica's and Beth's choices are certainly not right for everyone. What sets them apart, in addition to their lack of guilt, is the support system they've put into place. Few working women have Beth's stay-at-home husband, fully committed to his wife's career. "My husband was very happy, he had no conflict."

Each of these workaholic mothers is comfortable with her choice. Although they differ on the value of quality time, they make the same point about happy children: if the mother is happy, the children will be happy.

What sets Jewish women apart may well be, as Beth observed, that Judaism's traditional role for mothers presents an "insurmountable conflict." Indeed, the Hartmans' research finds "that Jewish women were more apt to stay out of the labor force longer with their preschool children than counterparts in the wider population." Thus the Jewish conflict starts early.

Working a demanding job intensifies the guilt and stress. Add to that Judaism's enormous pressure on educational achievement. Indeed, Jewish mothers often feel compelled to supplement their children's school life with enrichment programs, extra tutoring, and music/tennis/dance classes. Then there are Hebrew lessons, bar/bat mitzvahs, and confirmation schedules. Enough to make any working woman tremble.

In chapter 3, you'll meet two women who took on the added burden of *intermarriage*; a Catholic woman who converted to Judaism when she got married and a Jewish woman who married the son of a Baptist minister. Both women are earnestly trying to cushion their children from religious confusion.

Can they do it?

3

INTERMARRIAGE

LAUREN

SUSAN

Half a century ago, intermarriage was so frowned on that any Jew who married a Gentile was considered a pariah. Some parents, devout and observant, even declared their child dead for marrying outside the faith. They sat shiva. Intermarriage was deemed a betrayal, a slap in the face of everything Jews held dear, an abandonment of their religious and cultural identity. Worse, intermarriage was an invitation to convert, or to raise Christian children. A *shanda*. Shame, shame, shame.

Now count the number of mixed marriages you know. Friends. Relatives. Colleagues. Adds up, doesn't it? We are witnessing a distinct change of attitude. How did this happen?

In general, Jewish assimilation was extremely successful. During the course of the twentieth century, Jews moved into the educational, occupational, and cultural institutions of mainstream Gentile America. As women went to college and joined the workforce, intermarriages increased. Despite the sermons of rabbis and the consternation of Jewish leaders, "marrying out," once considered an affront to God, became more widely accepted. The hope was that the children of these marriages would be raised Jewish.

I'm sure you've heard the current lament, often offered with a shrug, "We *hope* he marries a Jewish girl. But if not, we only want him to be happy." Happiness, that most cherished secular goal, has become important in Jewish homes. Many intermarriages were happy ones. So the ban was softened.

In fact, *The Jewish Environmental Scan Toward the Year* 2000 predicted that "Intermarriage will continue at a high rate of over 50 percent and receive acquiescence." Some claim that rate could climb to 70 percent and few of the children born to these unions will be raised as Jews. "Intermarried couples with children will continue as the fastest growing household type," the *Scan* predicts. Clearly, many Americans view being Jewish as "membership in a cultural or ethnic group, rather than a religious one."

Indeed, more rabbis are now performing intermarriages and accepting non-Jews who wish to study for conversion. And some synagogues are offering classes to help intermarried couples resolve stressful holiday and in-law issues.

According to an article in *Hadassah Magazine*, the typical "Jew by choice," a common term for converts, is a woman married to a man whose Jewish life was limited to attending synagogue on the High Holidays and lighting Hanukkah candles. It is the wife's discovery of Judaism that draws her husband back to synagogue involvement, perhaps because her entrance into Judaism is through sustained religious training by rabbis, not through birth. Ironically, she may become more observant than her born-Jewish husband.

Such is the case of Lauren. Born Catholic, she chose to convert to Judaism and to raise her children Jewish, and she tells us why.

Lauren

LAUREN, 43, is exuberant, funny, and loud. She speaks her mind, her opinions are decisive, and she doesn't suffer fools lightly. Don't try to push in front of her in a checkout line. Typical New York Jew, right? Wrong.

Lauren was born into an Italian Catholic family. "Pasta every night and espresso all day." So marrying a Jew was a problem.

"My mother couldn't understand how a woman raised Catholic, who went through Catholic schools, would make that choice. And in my heart I thought, how could I have a child and not baptize him?"

Married to an attorney, Lauren is the mother of a son, 10, and a daughter, 7. Though she is now a stay-at-home mom, she once held a glamorous position as controller at Saks Fifth Avenue, a high-pressure job she loved.

Then how did this petite blond go from Catholic to Jewish, from career woman to full-time mommy, and from bustling Manhattan to the Jersey burbs?

"I had a B.S. in political science and wanted to go to law school. But the books were way too heavy, right?" she jokes. "So I figured, hey, why not try the fashion industry? I got an interview at Saks through a fashion designer friend, and I got the job. Entry level, but I worked my way up."

Lauren loves being Jewish. "It was very difficult to convert. But culturally, face it! Italians and Jews are all about family, food, and guilt. And phone calls and butting in on your life. It was all so comfortable, a good fit."

FIRST WE WENT *through the whole craziness of how to have a wedding. Rabbi alone? Priest alone? Both? The priest wanted us to agree to raise our children Catholic. The rabbi just asked me if I would convert. I said, "No, not at this moment, and if that's an absolute, we aren't getting married." I was twenty-eight, I wasn't closing the door, but I needed to think about it.*

My husband's parents weren't thrilled, either. But you have to know this family. The oldest daughter married two non-Jewish men. The first, she called her parents from the side of the road when she was nineteen

and said, "I'm getting married in a few minutes." The second, she said,
"Mom, I'm pregnant, can we use your backyard for a wedding?"
The second daughter is a lesbian.

*So when my husband came home and said he was in love, they wanted
to know, number one, Is it a woman? and two, Is she Jewish?*

*When we met each other, we clicked right away! I met my mother-in-
law on Sunday, she was at the store Wednesday. We had a lot in common: we both danced; I was in retail, she loved to shop.*

*When I was pregnant with my first child at thirty-one, I had a miscar-
riage and I started thinking seriously about how we were going to raise
children. Not that I felt God was punishing me, but I needed to do a lot
of soul-searching. I was very upset. And I started this journey, my husband and I both. We went to conversion school, which was actually for
people who wanted to find out more about Judaism. We studied with
three rabbis, went through a lot of courses, almost two years. And when I
was nine months pregnant, just before my son was born, I converted.*

*Holidays? I do Thanksgiving because it's benign. Both families, thirty
people, everybody comes, everybody's happy. My mother comes to Hanukkah. Friday night we have challah and candles; she comes, she
knows the prayers. And on Saturdays we go to synagogue as a family, the
four of us.*

*A Christmas tree? No. That was a tough decision. A lot of people have
a hard time giving that up. We celebrate the Jewish holidays, but on
Christmas we go to my aunt or my mother. I have to be very diplomatic.
Like one Easter my mother asked me to have Easter and I said, "No,
Mom, but come on Sunday"—it was my son's birthday. I did not have
ham and this is not a kosher house. I had pasta, I had turkey. And what
does she do? Brings a six-foot-high Easter basket with chocolate bunnies.
No one got offended. My kids were thrilled.*

*My children have no doubt what they are. I do not want them to be
confused. So no, we do not have a Christmas tree. We do not do any
Christian holidays. But I will go to my parents' house, I do that for respect. Also I don't want to hear her on the phone 150,000 times. Yes, both
my kids will be bar and bat [mitzvah]. Absolutely.*

I loved retail. I worked my way up and I ended up in the financial end. I was a controller, working directly under the president of the company, which was a wonderful experience. I worked with the buyers, I went to fashion shows, I was in the market, and I did a lot in the merchandising end. It was crazy during fashion week, always negotiating for money. Stressful, very stressful, very tough.

I was at Saks when I met my husband. He was right out of law school and decided law was not for him, so he went into the family business. I was making more than him. One of the things that attracted him was this great job I had, this powerful businesswoman I was. It was very exciting for him, very stimulating. He would come into the store, see they needed signatures, they needed my *approval. He loved it, everyone knew who I was. Even in the hospital having the miscarriage, I was talking on the phone, I couldn't separate myself. Tragic. I was thinking about the store.*

It changed almost immediately when my son was born. We had a sublet in Manhattan across from the New School. I ended up getting asthma very badly. But I wanted to stay in Manhattan. My husband wanted suburbia, no ifs, ands, or buts, suburbia—a community for raising children. I loved the excitement of New York. I can still walk there and feel the pulse of the city; it's the heartbeat of the world as far as I'm concerned. I've been to London, Paris. . . . New York is just to me the most exciting city in the world. But it all changed when our son was born!

They handed me this little bundle with beautiful blond hair and I said, "Hey wait, this could not be my child." I expected my husband's dark curly hair. I had a C-section which was long and hard because I was toxic and very sick. But once they handed me this baby, every pore, every cell, every part of my being fell in love. I felt it. I was in love, in love. And I remember my mother saying, "If you have to make a horrific choice—your child or your spouse—you will never choose your spouse." I know this now. If it's a matter of something for him or for them, the children win out. And it's interesting because my husband likes it that way.

He also liked the money I earned and thought I was going back. Saks was a wonderful place to work. They gave me six months off with two and a half months' full pay. I was constantly in touch with the store and my assistant would mail stuff to me.

I went back after four months because at that point my boss wanted me back. And when my assistant told me another executive was eyeing my corner office, I said, "Grrrr, I'm going back!"

But the morning I left—oh, it was awful. I was still nursing, which was another tough thing, and I was lucky to have an office to pump in and save the milk. I had a refigerator and I'd bring [the milk] home to feed the baby. It was tough even with my mother-in-law and my mother coming over, sharing this baby.

I lasted two weeks.

I had a 7:30 A.M. appointment, I left 6:30. We were now living in New Jersey. I had not nursed him and I felt engorged. I didn't get home till he was asleep. I hadn't seen him all day. It was horrible! So I said, "I don't know if I can do this." I had another meeting the next morning and I couldn't call home because I was smack in the middle of hectic. I loved the fast pace, I loved being pushed into a corner and digging out. But now it scared me.

I remember coming home and saying, "I love this job but I can't do everything—do the job right and then come home and do the parent-ing." Because when I was with my son, I was totally with him. I nursed him, I loved it. It was that raw, all-consuming love. And when the phone rang and I had to put him down because it was the store, it was such a conflict.

I felt like I was being ripped apart. I felt guilty to the store and guilty to my son. I interviewed for some part-time jobs and I decided to stay home. My husband would be the breadwinner. He was doing well.

What I didn't know is that I'd have a son with a disability. My son is attention-deficit hyperactive, ADHD. Three years later my daughter was born. My choice not to work was the right one. Absolutely.

When you have an ADHD child, he's all over the place and he's clas-sified as handicapped. A tough thing to hear. He was in a preschool pro-gram and they did a beautiful job, but it takes a lot. You have follow-

through with what the occupational therapists tell you, specific motor skills, speech therapists, a lot of things to do. He takes a lot of time.

I attacked everything I could get my hands on about ADHD. We saw many therapists, alternative everythings, diets. I'm like a maven on hyperactivity.

When it comes to my son, if I wasn't there, I don't think he would have turned out quite the way he is now. He's in a full mainstream class and that's because I was a full-time mother. Yes. And not just me. My husband is extremely involved. He does his parenting really well. He's 100 percent. He can't do the carpooling and all the other after-school stuff, but he is there for homework and Hebrew. My mother told me, "Do not marry an Italian. The wandering eye, domineering." My husband is the opposite.

And I have a lot of friends. I am so blessed. I have tons of girlfriends and I go out with a lot of them. My girlfriends and I do a lot together. We have Girls' Night Out—we go out four, five girls. We laugh, we talk, we drink. A terrific time. [They talk] about their husbands, how they expect a lot. Some of my friends are going back part time. Me, I'd start out part time and it would get all-consuming.

I do a lot of PTA work, I'm on the cultural arts board, I chair a lot of leadership programs for the Jewish community. Some [women] have the type of career they can juggle. Not the job I had. I feel very lucky. [But] if I needed the money, my ideas might be very different.

There's so much joy in parenting, also so much pain. And when you have a child with a disability, it takes a lot of work. There are days I miss the business world and the stimulation.

Women who say they have it all really don't, they pay the price. I think everybody pays a price. When you stay home, you pay a price. [Because] in America, you are what you do. People ask, "What do you do?" Staying home, you're not valued.

I think Jewish women are more intense about these issues. I try not to judge people by their nationality and genetics, but I find Jewish women feel more guilt-ridden if they shortchange their children or perceive it that way. Absolutely.

And with a Jewish upbringing, you ask, "What do I do with all this ed-ucation now that I have children?" It's important to procreate and keep the Jewishness alive, yes. But what about the other part, the part that you worked so hard to achieve? Education, education! It's instilled in you. So if you don't work, you feel guilty. I worked in the business world. Then I put on the Mommy hat. I know.

I just did my twenty-fifth high school reunion, and I saw a lot of women were working because they had to financially. So I felt spoiled. They were appalled that I gave up my position and wanted to stay home with my kids. Maybe I'm really self-centered. From eight-thirty to three, that's my time. But after that, my day begins and I'm in the car from three o'clock nonstop; drop off, pick up, drop off, group therapy, Hebrew school, speech therapy, to eight, nine o'clock. I can't imagine anyone doing it like me, you can't pay to have that done.

A lot of Jewish women expect well . . . traveling, owning a second home; it's very status oriented. And I don't think that's so bad. You work hard, you want nice things.

I think if you can do both parenting and business and really feel good about it, it's great!

I'm thrilled that I'm able to stay home. Not all fun and games, but I wouldn't change it.

Lauren converted to Judaism after several years of study, and she is ded-icated to bringing her children up Jewish. To avoid religious confu-sion, she refused to have a Christmas tree. But, on Christian holidays she visits her parents out of respect. Lauren shows us that some inter-marriages can work with minimal stress.

Lauren is helped by a keen sense of humor. Flexible and realistic, she's not offended when her Catholic mother brings her Jewish chil-dren a six-foot-high Easter basket. Instead of starting World War III, she is amused.

She also admits she's thrilled to stay at home. Without her constant supervision, her ADHD son would not have turned out so well. She's proud of that accomplishment. She tells us how she "fell in love" with her child. How her intention to return to work crumbled after two weeks of juggling parenting and full-time work. How she felt "ripped apart," guilty about her job and guilty about her son. And she made her choice.

You have to admire this woman. She refused conversion as a prerequisite to intermarriage and came to Judaism her way: through study and commitment. Burdened with the stress of her child's disability, she enlisted her husband who "did his parenting well." And she refused to bow to the view that staying home was a foolish decision. "My choice not to work was the right one. Absolutely!"

Strong-willed and self-confident, Lauren points out that "everyone pays a price." She is the stay-at-home mother who lost status at her high school reunion, the powerful businesswoman who gave up her glamorous job in Manhattan for carpooling in the burbs. But she has no regrets. It was right for her. Like the workaholic mothers in chapter 2, Lauren is convinced she made the right choice.

Susan

SUSAN, 41 and born Jewish, is married to the son of a minister; her husband did *not* accept conversion to Judaism. And yes, they *do* have a Christmas tree.

Susan has two terrific kids, a modest house in Pennsylvania, and a close and loving intermarriage. How did they negotiate their differences? Why is it working for them when other intermarriages end in divorce? Susan tells us how she constructed it: carefully, one step at a time.

Smiling, she greets me at the front door. She wears sneakers and a sweat suit that does not conceal her thin, girlish frame. With her gentle blue eyes, blond curly hair, and washed-clean face, she could pass for a college student.

We step over toys and books and puzzles, then sit down around her kitchen table. Her split-level home, in a suburb of Philadelphia, is neat but child centered. She pours us mugs of steaming coffee.

Married twelve years, with a son, 7, and a daughter, 3, Susan earned a bachelor's degree in psychology and an M.S.W. in mental health. Her first job was a demanding full-time appointment working in a psychiatric day program that focused on the retarded. Why? Her grandmother and her mother's brother, Steve, who had Down's syndrome, both lived with them. Both were influences.

In the 1960s, Susan and her divorced mom, Grandma Sarah, and Uncle Steve were not your typical nuclear family. Married now to a midwestern Baptist from Cedar Springs, Michigan, Susan and her husband are active members of a Reconstructionist synagogue.

"My husband sings in the choir, he has a beautiful voice, and I'm also very involved in our synagogue. But he did *not* convert." She makes that clear.

IN HIGH SCHOOL, *I spent a couple of summers at a Jewish day camp, and I joined an Orthodox youth group although I was bat mitzvahed in a Conservative synogogue.*

Then at sixteen, I went on a trip to Israel and it gave me a strong Jewish identification separate from the ritual. I became more Zionist and less religious, more interested in Russian Jews and political action.

My parents divorced when I was a baby and my grandmother lived with us. Also my mother's brother, Uncle Steve, who was Down's syndrome. What influenced me strongly is what my grandmother did for him and the impact she had on developing his potential. She saw to it that he had a quality life living with us. She even had a playground built in our backyard so the other kids would play with him. She was very much an advocate. She'd talk with the governor about the state institution, and she'd bring kids home for Christmas.

My husband and I became friends first: we were colleagues at work. He grew up in the Midwest. His father was a very conservative Baptist minister in Cedar Springs, Michigan. He saw his first movie at eighteen. No movies, no playing cards, no dancing, no drinking, no smoking, no sex, nothing! He never met a Jew until he was seventeen and his family moved to West Palm Beach, Florida. He went to a small Christian college, near Buffalo, with the reputation that it was located one hour from the nearest sin. That was his background. In college he married a Christian girl—it was the only way you could have sex. He was twenty-one; it didn't last. No children.

We were not public when we started dating because my boss was Orthodox and couldn't understand why anyone wasn't Orthodox. Had I known then what I know now, I would have sued his butt off for sexual harassment. He'd close the door, and tell me how attracted he was to me. He'd hit on me, this father of five.

By this time my husband was going to a Mennonite church [which] was doing a lot of social action. It opened him up and he moved away from the "no movies" stuff. We moved in together and we got marrried when we were both twenty-eight.

He always knew it was important for me to raise my kids Jewish, and he was okay with that because there was a certain respect for Jewish people— the chosen people—and he said there was nothing in Judaism that conflicted with Christianity. He is very well versed in the Old Testament.

Neither of us had any desire for the other person to convert. I would be Jewish, he would be Christian.

Most people start synagogue-shopping when they have kids. We did it before we even got married. We visited a Reconstructionist synagogue and, that same Sunday, a Mennonite church.

A lot of rabbis wouldn't marry us. Then we heard about one who would. She was ordained by the Reconstructionists and we both really liked her. He was fine with having a Jewish wedding, and my mother really liked him and liked that we'd be married by a rabbi and raise Jewish children. His parents didn't attend. The excuse was, living in Florida they didn't have warm clothes. But his sisters and brothers came.

One of the reasons we joined this synagogue was they were very welcoming of non-Jewish spouses. It's right in their by-laws and they have a very high percentage of interfaith couples, maybe 30 percent to 40 percent. Nine years ago we started an Interfaith Couple Support Group and our group still meets. We talk about negotiating the holidays and how to raise our kids, and we meet once a month.

We're very involved. Our son had a bris, he goes to Sunday school, and he'll be bar mitzvahed. Our daughter had a baby-naming. They are clear on who they are. On Friday night, we light candles, we have challah, we say the blessings. They are Jewish children.

I was working as director of program development when my son was born. Writing proposals and doing marketing. I was fulltime with benefits and I enjoyed it. So I took off three months with the idea I'd return to work part time for six months and then go back full time. I didn't have an office, I was going to a hospital or somewhere else—and they bought me a computer to work at home. I was on the road, trying to do full time in part-time hours. Then I went back full time and put my son in daycare.

The juggling was okay until my daughter was born.

I took the same maternity leave arrangement. But when I came back part time, the pressure was awful to go full time. And there was a different CEO, very stressful, and no respect for me. They espoused family values, sure, but they gave you very little support. Maternity leave and flexitime look good on paper, but you get screwed over when you come back to work.

I put my daughter in daycare, but I was feeling miserable, miserable. I'd nurse her in the baby room on my lunch hour, going from one meeting to another.

The pivotal moment came when I registered my son for kindergarten. It just hit me, that being with them was such a time-limited opportunity. I spoke to my husband and he got assurances that his job was secure. So he said okay, leave. I needed a break. And we decided that even if we had to use savings, we should. So I left. She was ten months. I took her out of daycare and left my job. It was June.

In August, my husband's company got bought out and he had no job. It was scary, very scary.

Through networking and old contacts I picked up free-lance work, and

I developed my own marketing and public relations work. I did bro-chures, all part time at home, and we managed. My mother was retired and she moved down here to be near us. If I had a phone meeting or something I had to do, she'd come over. I'm really grateful to her. A year later my husband landed a good job and I continued to do my work at home. So we were okay.

Once, I asked my husband what kind of Christmas dinner did he have growing up, and he said "We never really had one." It was unfathomable to me! A major holiday without food? Not for Jewish people. [There's] the importance of food and preparing. So I invited interfaith couples for Christmas and I put out a buffet, an open house. My mother always did that. The idea of preparing food and having enough food, that's defi-nitely a Jewish thing. You have a veggie coming, you make something special for them. So we have Christmas dinner for him. And Rosh Ha-shanah dinner, too.

We also have a Christmas tree—it's become one of our traditions. The kids are very clear they are Jewish, it's not an issue, no confusion. They have a strong Jewish identity. They say, "Daddy's Christian," and other people we know are in the same boat, so we talk about it. We exchange Christmas gifts and Hanukkah gifts. We have both.

In our town, our son is the only Jewish kid in the class. We have an Easter egg hunt and it's a fun thing, not religious. It doesn't feel like a conflict for us.

I think there'd be friction if I decided unilaterally, "this year we're not having a Christmas tree." My husband takes off from work for Rosh Ha-shanah and Yom Kippur. We do a seder, and he doesn't like us to do the short version.

My husband comes from such a WASP family; we joke that in his fam-ily you have to pry an opinion out of them. In my family and in our fam-ily there's talk, talk, talk and our kids are loud at the dinner table. How he grew up, one person spoke at a time. No interruptions. Then silence. Cul-turally, it's very different. Jews are opinionated, we speak up.

Jewish women also tend to be high achievers. It's hard to work all the career and family pieces in. Jewish women like to work in their own businesses, to call the shots, and be able to block off time for their kids. They're juggling time. And some have stepped back to part time like me.

The biggest challenge is time, making good use of it. The kids first, of course, but I have to work because we need the money. Our car has 150,000 miles and the air-conditioner broke. We need a van. But it can wait. Time is more important to me than having a lot of things. We have everything we need and a lot of things we want. The other stuff can wait.

What's hard is to find couple time and couple energy. It's hard to go out by ourselves, so my husband is shortchanged. We're focused on the kids—it's hard to carve time out for each other.

I like being a milk-and-cookies mom. In the morning and naptime is when I work. I meet the bus and that's when I hear about my son's day, that's when it's fresh. If he sits on the sidewalk with his backpack to tell me about recess, I know what's going on, not a babysitter. And I try to give him time when she's napping. I'm always juggling time. Time for his snack, time to look at his homework. I try to squeeze out individual time for each child.

Looking back, I see that I was very drawn to be with my kids and the job was getting more and more stressful. So it was easy to leave.

Will I go back full time when they're both in school? I don't know. My goal is to build up my business, but to stay at home. There's going to be sick days and I'll still want to go on their school trips.

I was a high achiever. I had a lot of professional goals. I achieved some of them. But I was disillusioned with corporate life and the politics of it. Work stopped being a passion for me.

My family is my passion.

It turned out very different than I expected.

Is it heresy for intermarried couples raising Jewish children to cele-brate Christian holidays? Many couples grapple with that issue. Susan, born Jewish, has a Christmas tree. Lauren, born Catholic, does not. Susan is comfortable making a Christmas buffet for intermarried couples, and her children understand that daddy is Christian. Does that make her less Jewish than Lauren, a convert to Judaism?

What these women have in common is that they have resolved their interfaith conflicts *to the satisfaction of themselves and their spouses.* Each respects her spouse's background and accommodates those differences. They view differences as cultural, rather than religious. They are not hard-liners, belligerent or unyielding, out to prove they are right.

What pious Jews fear most is that by making cultural adjustments, Judaism will be watered down and the religion so compromised it will be lost. Jews in intermarriages will discard their religious obligations in order to avoid marital conflict. Result? Judaism, strictly observed, will fall by the wayside.

In secular, multicultural America, interfaith marriages ignite valid fears. In addition to the fear of the death of Judaism as a religion, there is the fear of divorce, with children torn apart and emotionally damaged.

So why is it working for Susan when there are so many obstacles in the way?

For one thing, Susan is clear about raising her children Jewish and so is her husband. Both accepted Reconstructionism because the synagogue was welcoming to intermarriages. Rabbi Dan Ehrenkrantz of Reconstructionist B'nai Keshet in Montclair, New Jersey, told me that Reconstructionists are "socially closer to Reform Jews and slightly more observant than Conservatives." In 1998, there were only ninety-eight congregations in this country, a tiny percentage, creating "an atmosphere of acceptance for mixed marriages." *Acceptance makes life easier.*

Suppose Susan had *not* found Reconstructionism? We can only speculate what conflicts might have arisen and what alternative choices might have been made. Some observers of intermarriages simply sigh and say, "Thank God the children are Jewish." Others remain adamant: intermarriage spells the death of Judaism.

Susan's story appears to belie that prediction. Instead of battles over who wins, she and her husband attend a monthly support group that tackles the sticky questions of holidays and in-laws. There is good will, not holier-than-thou attitudes, and this turns the heat down on incendiary issues. Even the Christmas tree question, a hot button in most mixed marriages, is defused. She and her children are Jewish. Daddy's Christian. What is working for them is that both parents give the same message. Respect for differences. A united front. A welcoming community.

For Susan, more stressful than religion was the workplace.

Her company espoused family values, but hassled her to come back to work full time. So she chose to leave and to work from home. With the computer revolutionizing the workplace, there are more choices. For Susan, material possessions were less important than time with her family. Elizabeth Perle McKenna's book *When Work Doesn't Work Anymore* confirms that time and flexibility are more important than money when you are balancing work and love.

Finally, Susan and Lauren show us a changing attitude toward religious differences. Holidays can be celebrated as *cultural* events respecting the non-Jewish spouse's religion. Lauren's Catholic mom even attends Hanukkah and sabbath at Lauren's home.

Today, America's public schools include multicultural events as part of their curricula. Children are taught respect for other religions and the emphasis is on ethnic celebrations, not religious observances best left to families.

With one million intermarried couples coping with the endless struggles of holidays, December can become the cruelest month. But neither Susan's children nor Lauren's children seem confused. Both marriages seem in good shape. Not easy to achieve.

The desire to raise a family without religious confusion seems paramount among intermarried couples. In fact, many converted Jews say they want their children to marry Jews. As the children of converted Jews become "born Jews," will the twenty-first century see a redefining of American Judaism? Or will we see its disappearance?

Now that we've looked at religious women, workaholics, and intermarriages, let's look at women with *attitude*. In the next chapter you'll meet three women who hold strong opinions and aren't afraid to live by their principles. I call them *political women*. A lobbyist, a lawyer, and a lesbian activist.

4

POLITICAL

WOMEN

AMY

RONA

TRACY

My mother often told me when I was a child, "You have a Big Mouth." Her voice was stern, but her hazel eyes held a twinkle of pride so I didn't take it as a put-down. I understood that a Big Mouth had a certain value. We call it chutzpah.

Here are three women with chutzpah. They are spiritual daughters of Emma Goldman and, though they haven't shouted political messages in Union Square, they believe in fighting injustice and working to effect change. Gentle, mild, and diffident is not their style. Indeed, the image of Jewish women perpetuated in movies and television is often that of women like them: opinionated, outspoken, and feisty. Sometimes even abrasive.

Take Fran Drescher's 1993 televison debut as Nanny Fine. Joyce Antler, editor of *Talking Back*, points out that what made the program work was "the premise of culture clash." Nasal, whining, Jewish Fran against proper, uptight Maxwell Sheffield. The fun of the show was the shtick watching gaudy Fran outwit her adversaries. Fran had chutzpah. And the show ran until 1999 despite objections about Jewish female stereotypes: overeating, overdressing, and overspending. Fran Fine was more than a caricature of a Jewish woman: she was the hero of her own life.

This chapter introduces three women with chutzpah.

AMY is a political lobbyist uprooted from New York to St. Louis, Missouri. RONA is a litigator who defends Mafia figures and works for women's issues. TRACY is cochair of B'YACHAD, a gay/lesbian network, and she's planning to have a baby with her partner. All three share a fierce commitment to social change.

Amy

AMY, 53, is married and the mother of one adult daughter. Originally from Denver and raised in a kosher Orthodox home, she's been relocated many times by her husband's corporation.

From Denver they were moved to New York, where she held the job of statistician for CBS News. Then Amy's family, along with two hundred other families, was moved again—this time to St. Louis, Missouri. Culture shock for most of the New Yorkers, but not for Amy. St. Louis was reminiscent of Denver, a small midwestern city with a comfortable Jewish community and a much slower pace of life.

However, she found St. Louis families were not very welcoming to outsiders. "They hang out with their high school—no, their kindergarten—friends, and you're not one of them and never will be." Nevertheless, Amy was a political animal with an adaptive spirit.

Blond and fresh-looking, with her hair pulled back in a ponytail, she's smart and savvy, a math major with a master's in statistics. She put in a fifteen-year stint with the U.S. Bureau of the Census. Today she works as a very active lobbyist for civil rights and Jewish causes.

SIX YEARS AGO I *made the move to St. Louis for my husband. I was not happy. In New York, I was working at CBS News doing election night estimations as a statistician. A great job, and it was good for my career. I came screaming and kicking to New York from Denver and ended up in this dream job on the* New York Times *poll and gained an additional background. And this political experience helped me get my job when we moved again to St. Louis.*

By then, our daughter was a junior in college, but she still claims we abandoned her. I felt bad because we had uprooted her in fifth grade, too, and it took her two years to acclimate.

I approached the moves positively. But in St. Louis my skills did not apply, even with the relocation firm helping spouses find jobs. So I took a market research job on contract for two years and I was not happy.

They were very anti–New York and anti Jew and I was the New York Jew there. They were twenty year olds, I was late forties. I kept hearing, "I knew a Jew once." And on a professional level, the market research was a bastardized use of statistics. The client wanted an outcome, they'd make sure they got it. Morally, ethically, and personally, I was uncomfortable.

One day I was at a meeting and I reminded them, "Don't forget to vote, it's election day." And they came down on me. "Don't tell us what to do and don't drop your politics on us!" I was astonished by the apathy. I decided to make a career change.

When the contract was over, I became active in local politics and worked on a couple of campaigns. I became known in the community and I worked with my local representative to the state legislature. She wanted to retire and she tapped me to be her replacement. She was seventy-six, the only Jewish legislator, and she wanted a Jewish replacement. However, I'd have to [live] in Jefferson City, the state capital, Monday through Thursday. Also, running for political office you have to do a lot of fundraising and begging for money. My husband and I talked it over and the negatives won. I decided against it.

At the same time I was doing something for myself, going to graduate school at Washington University. And I just got my master's in political science, and that's so satisfying.

In St. Louis, there's tremendous pressure for women of my generation not to work. It's different for young women in today's marketplace, but women my age were not working. To be comfortable in the community I had to do something outside of the workforce. So I opted to become very active in political organizations and Jewish organizations.

I'm on the board of directors of the JCC [Jewish Community Center]— —that's quite an honor to be asked—and I work for [the] National Council of Jewish Women. And my favorite is the American Jewish Committee [AJC]. I was fortunate to be invited; it was an excellent fit because they knew my political background. The top tier of Jewish St. Louis is part of this wonderful organization and I'm now the vice president. And I go back and forth to Washington and Jefferson City, lobbying for them on both Jewish and civil rights issues.

Right now the biggest issue coming to vote next Tuesday is concealed handguns, and we're lobbying against it. It's a voters' issue on the ballot. The other issue is an advocacy forum for AJC representatives, and senators come to talk to us. It's closed out to the media, no one taking notes. Republicans, Democrats, and Independents. Through this, I've become known in Jefferson City.

I've always [felt] change is good. St. Louis was good to me. My days are full. Life is exciting.

What all this has evolved to is that it's a career. Politics and Jewish issues, both dear to my heart.

Political action is Amy's arena. She loves being in the heart of a debate, loves the excitement of feeling she can make a difference, loves the challenge of crossing swords.

Uprooting her family while balancing her own work as a statistician, she decided to leave a job she disliked and to became a full-time lobbyist. Outspoken and effective, she is a Big Mouth (to use my mother's words) in a long line of feisty Jewish women.

A few days after this interview took place, I opened the *New York*

Times and read the results of Amy's lobbying against concealed hand-guns: "Missouri Rejects Bid to Allow Concealed Guns." The article described the statewide defeat of the National Rifle Association (NRA), which had spent close to four million dollars and had sent actor Charlton Heston on frequent visits to the state on its behalf. However, despite the NRA's efforts, lobbyists like Amy defeated the proposal. She made a difference.

I phoned her and she was jubilant.

Rona

RONA, 46, is a litigator who defends both Mafia figures and women battling discrimination. Confusing? She doesn't think so.

It's early afternoon when I pull up to a Victorian house that is her office. It's not your ordinary lawyer's office. And the raven-haired attorney sitting cross-legged behind her desk is not your ordinary lawyer. She's wearing cowboy boots and a sexy sweater and her bike is propped against the fireplace wall.

Married twelve years, with two stepchildren, 16 and 17, she's not in a traditional marriage, either. Two residences, his and hers: she lives in an apartment near her office; he and the kids live down the Jersey Shore. They rendezvous on weekends. She was raised in a Conservative Jewish home; her grandparents started a temple in Newark. But after her bat mitzvah, "the religious aspects of Judaism didn't hold my interest."

However, in 1983, after losing a death penalty case, she visited Israel and became a zealot. "My allegiance to Israel is political and philosophical." She came home feeling she had found a sense of belonging that was missing in her life.

She was brought up in a very monied, privileged household; her family employed a full-time cook, a cleaning person, and a nanny. "I didn't know what an ironing board was." Her parents split up when she was sixteen. "Their divorce made me *never* want to get married. In fact, my marriage is a fluke."

Rona describes herself as a devoted feminist.

I BELIEVE VERY *strongly in empowerment, in women's issues, and women's causes. Money, to me, is empowerment. It's not necessarily running for office, but it's funding for women who run for office. That's what I'm doing. It took a long damn time to make as much money as a man. That's it: money is empowerment!*

My life is glamorous and fascinating; I'm living a dream life. There's no better husband, no goals I haven't achieved. I've pursued cases I wanted—sometimes at a fourth of my hourly rate—but I'm against the death penalty and the government killing people. It's my job to fight it in the courtroom. I try what people think are the worst crimes. I represented the Jewish guy who killed his two kids because his wife was going to convert them to Catholic. I saved his life and he died a year later of cancer.

As a public defender, I worked six, seven years and established myself in the press. In 1986, I was fascinated by organized crime and I established a following. People approached me to represent the accused heads of crime families, the capos, caporegines, the captains. The don is the patriarch. I believe I was the first woman in the country to represent an accused family, the De Cavalcante crime family, also known as Sam the Plumber back in the old days of Newark. I represented John Riggi. I had drivers and Christmas cookies; they treated me kindly.

He's in jail now. He pleaded guilty of racketeering, being the head of an organized crime family, extortion, bribery, violence to get kickbacks. A two-month trial. It was fun, a short part of my life. I met the important people, they're all in jail now. The sons and daughters are taking over, [but] I won't be defending them because there are drugs involved. No, I've never been scared. They were conscientious about paying my bills. Wonderful people; they treated me well and respectfully.

I never wanted children. If I had had kids to raise, I wouldn't have what I have now. And in law school I tell the young women, "I'm forty-six, and you can't do it all, it's a lie!" If you want to succeed at parenting or a full-time career, fine. I believe it's impossible to do both."

As a feminist, I never thought I would say that. For me, I need to work six days a week to achieve what I want to do. I've done it for twenty years now and I don't know how to stop. I love what I do. It's how I feel I change the world. So I don't regret not having children, not for an instant.

I have wonderful step-children. My husband's a practicing Catholic, church every Sunday. I go occasionally, but I don't participate and his kids probably know more about Judaism than Catholicism. My husband's a nonpracticing attorney, a manufacturer of vinegar. He's the one raising the children. He does the laundry, he feeds them, the home-work, their activities—he's Mr. Mom. I thought his children would inter-fere with my lifestyle. Every prospective step-parent better think damn long about it.

My words are this: if you want to succeed in the fullest in either pa-renting or career, you can't *balance them equally. That doesn't knock feminism; there are housewives who are feminists. There are feminists who try to do both, and they'll tell you they're shortchanging their [children], they feel guilty. I can't work feeling guilty, I need full con-centration. [So] when [women] say to me, "I want to have kids and I want to be a famous lawyer," I say, "Fine. Hire somebody to take care of your children. You won't raise them, that's your choice." This is about* choices.

My choice—from the first cry in the crib I knew it—was to pursue the career. I was lucky to find a family that accepted me and my ambi-tions. I am an opportunist, I take every opportunity to self-advance. I don't step on people, but I know my step-daughter will have it easier after I leave.

As a political person, I believe I can change the world. That's my pas-sion, my reason for waking up. I have a lot of energy; my mind starts going at four in the morning, I'm jogging by five. I work out, I ride horses, I jump horses, I ballroom dance with my husband, I lift weights.

What I enjoy most is quiet time, Friday night to Sunday with my hus-band, just hanging out. I travel a lot, I try cases in other states. They like the excitement of my balancing act. [But] I make compromises for the family. If they call me to come down, I get my sweet cheeks down if they're needy. And there are political affairs I miss on the weekends.

I'm past president of the Association of Criminal Defense Lawyers and the first woman president. And honored at New Jersey PAC [Performing Arts Center] for the Women's Fund of New Jersey. I work with battered women, abused children, reproductve rights. We started the Women's Fund with the imprimatur of Governor Whitman and we have it to a point where we get private funding from large corporations. The first year I threw my tenant out and gave them office space—my copier, secretary, fax. They took over my office for twelve months until I couldn't afford to shelter them.

I'm radical, I'm outspoken. I think women have settled for getting 75 cents on the dollar. I want 110 cents because I work harder, and that's radical! I say it everywhere. I speak my mind. To the governor, on commissions; and I talk about financially empowering women. It's about money! About earning power!

I'm pro-choice to the extreme; I call myself pro-abortion. Letting men decide is a very bad policy. I also believe, against Republican policies, in helping single women with children. We need to build our women up. We spent so many years tearing them down, putting them in a little niche—you are "mother," "daughter," "wife." I'm tired of it. I speak out all over the country. Are my politics radical? They are, they are. Would I defend Hitler? I just don't know.

At one point I felt I wasn't giving enough to the marriage, trying to balance it all; and I was miserable. Guilty is an understatement. So I decided to cut back on my public life. I call it my "coming home period." The best thing a woman can do is, don't bring your competitive harshness home. Friday night, I get there about seven, eight. I try to chill and it takes to Saturday afternoon, that's the truth. Self-confidence is the mask you wear; I take the mask off with my husband.

I'd like to see more women in office. I believe politics is a wonderful career for women. It can be part time and [you can] have a family. Women care about people [so] they should represent people. My stepdaughter, seventeen, is one tough broad and she's six foot one. I discourage her from law. I'd like [her] to have a less consuming career. A more rounded existence, a family life.

I've been asked to run for office and I went to a meeting to scope it out.

But I would never run for politics. You have to be on all the time, and you can't practice law and do both.

Jews are very family based, that's the conflict with having a full-time career. The other side is, Jews are very educated and ambitious. We savor education, and we feel guilty when we take away from family life. Every Jewish woman I know says, "I wish I had more time at home." Lamenting.

In ten years I see myself working on more boards, spending more time with my husband, and being a competitive horsewoman. I want to establish that balance we're all seeking.

According to a special report in *Vanity Fair*, the fields many women excel in "are politics, business, media, and higher education"—unreachable a few decades ago. Yet many bold women, like Rona, are unwilling to set themselves up for the rigors of public life. Is it the accompanying scrutiny that scares them off?

"You can't run for political office because they'll destroy you," said New York WOR radio talk-show host Joan Hamburg. Is this the reality? Rona says she doesn't want to be "*on all the time.*" I suspect she's unwilling to be roasted on the spit for her radical politics. She doesn't want her life dissected, her privacy invaded.

According to *Jews in America* (ed. Roberta Rosenberg Farber and Chaim Waxman), "Jews are the most liberal group in the country." Liberal on redistribution of income, civil rights for racial and ethnic minorities, and social justice for all. Clearly, Jewish values affect politics.

To some, Rona's life may seem unnatural. "I never wanted children." Regrets? "Not for an instant."

She is not alone.

Many career women don't even think about having children until they reach thirty to thirty-five. Although childbearing is optimal biologically in their early twenties, these women are too busy building careers. Some women choose a child-free existence as a way of optimizing their careers. Clearly, Rona's political mission takes precedence over her need for children.

Balancing work and children seems quite an impossible task to Rona. She insists that to succeed to the fullest, you can't do it all: "It's a lie." But she is aware her work-centered life won't appeal to everyone. She hopes her step-daughter will enjoy a more rounded existence and a family life.

Few women lawyers strive to achieve Rona's level of success. It costs too much. While her life is glamorous and fascinating, "a dream life," it could be a nightmare to women with families. We all know women lawyers who are balancing families and careers. They do not maintain separate households. They do not wait for Saturday to "chill."

Balancing work and families, they "chill" every evening when they come home from work and put dinner on the table. They raise children, they run households. Their life is not as exciting or dramatic as Rona's. Perhaps they even gave up business partnerships to factor in "wife" and "mommy." For those women, law still represents a viable career and an exciting challenge. A smart choice.

Most working women don't want to *be* Rona.

But we need people like Rona. We need mavericks, big mouths, and radicals.

Tracy

TRACY, 35, is lively and edgy. Her turquoise eyes match the arc of her turquoise ear-studs, and her hands flutter to make a point. Short and painfully thin, she wears sneakers, jeans, and granny glasses. She also wears a wedding ring. An adopted child who was born to WASPs, she and her partner, a Gentile woman, have been together four years.

Tracy holds a B.A. in Judaic studies, a master's in counseling, and a B.A. in nursing. Employed as a nurse at HIP, an HMO that went bankrupt, she is, at the moment, unemployed.

She was brought up in a secular home with a strong socialist and Workman's Circle background, where religion was *not* stressed. She learned Yiddish, not Hebrew. "We identified *ethnically*. Judaica was all over my mother's house, awareness of the Holocaust."

She spent a year in Israel after high school and another year there as a college senior. As a nurse, she worked in the burn unit of St. Barnabas Medical Center in New Jersey, which was "the greatest challenge I ever had to balancing work, love, and life." She tells us why.

I WAS WORKING nights 6 P.M. to 7 A.M., and I felt like I was walking around with a permament hangover. My partner was working days, so we rarely saw each other. We're together four years. She works days as a secretary at a hospital and she has her own landscaping business, so our time was not quality time. We didn't argue, we'd clam up. Silence.

Is there a difference with lesbians? Well, women understand each other better; we pick up intuitively; we're both from Venus, so there's no power struggles. Our apartment is furnished in Early Garage Sale, we're not materialistic, and we don't fight about who's right or wrong. It's not about the win or lose thing, like straight couples.

I was in denial a long time. I was trying to date men. They were satisfied sexually, I was not. What happened is the first time I was with a woman, it was better than anything with a man. Also I didn't realize how unhappy I was until I fell in love with a very close friend, and we made it happen. I was twenty-one and I was very scared. I kept it a secret for years. Around twenty-eight, I came out to my parents.

[At college] the lesbians were active politically. Interestingly, at that time I didn't think being lesbian and Jewish could be compatible. I knew I couldn't be a member of Hadassah, that Judaism was heterosexually oriented. But [the campus] in 1982 had a very active gay community, posters all around—"Lesbians for Equal Rights." I was nineteen and struggling with my sexuality.

Are Jewish lesbians more outspoken? I don't know. I think Jews make more noise. Because we have a collective consciousness. We are always concerned with the perpetuation of our people. We are community focused, we're taught to better ourselves and mankind. Jewish women are more intense politically.

[Take] my family. My father marched in the civil rights movement, my

mom too. We all marched together in D.C. as a family against the war in Vietnam. My brother is a political lobbyist for environmental-friendly energy resources. He worked in the Clinton administration. And my sister is very political, she "overtook" the student union building [at Columbia] in 1975; it made the New York Times.

I've never been out to my employer; it's not something I say in an interview and no one can ask. But on the job if someone asks what does my husband do, I say, "My partner is a secretary." They get it.

As cochair of the Gay and Lesbian Network sponsored by the Jewish Family Services, I'm active politically. Our mission is to provide a safe, nurturing environment and increase awareness. We've spoken at B'nai B'rith and various temples about our experiences. We have monthly sabbath dinners where we meet other gays, and we have services and Purim parties, we go to museums. It's an outreach program for community education. We've gone to [a] Hebrew high school, but not public schools.

One Orthodox rabbi said, "Absolutely not, you can't speak unless there's an opposing view to say it's not okay to be gay." He thinks the Bible says it's a sin, an abomination. So our group is forming a response and we've invited him to come talk to us. Some synagogues are welcoming; the Orthodox is our hardest group.

Is homosexuality a lifestyle? A choice? I think our genetic makeup gives us dispositions to like or dislike certain things, we can't explain why. Something innate in us that causes us to respond. What makes me attracted to women more than men? I don't know, it's part of my genetic makeup. What we have a choice with is what we do with those feelings. I've heard of people who live their whole life in denial and try to make themselves straight. Go to psychoanalysis or go back to God. Well, I made a choice to go with my feelings.

Both my partner and I want to have kids, we'd like a family. These issues are definitely coming up. Where to do this? Fortunately we live in the New York area, the most liberal area in the country. But affording a family, owning a home, and paying for schools—it's very expensive. So we're thinking of moving. Our main concern is financial.

With straight couples, you wake up, you're pregnant. With us, one of us has to be inseminated. We talk about it. An anonymous donor? Adopt? It's pretty difficult even when you're straight. I think my partner will be the one to get pregnant. I'll have the full-time job, I'll be the breadwinner. We want one of us to be home, we've talked it through. Our ultimate fantasy is to combine work and love. She'll be the stay-at-home mom.

My partner is not Jewish and the religious *upbringing of this child is our struggle. She has a very stong Methodist upbringing. Our wedding was easier. We had a rabbi and a* huppa *and a lesbian minister. It was at a gay resort on a beautiful fall day. My grandmother and mother walked me down the aisle, her father walked her down. She celebrates our Jewish holidays. [But] it's hard for me to celebrate Christmas because I'm aware it's the birthday of Christ, whom I don't believe in. Having a Christmas tree is very uncomfortable; a little one, it's all I can deal with. Easter and the Resurrection; a lot of* religious *things to resolve.*

Politically, the main issue [for us] is legal *recognition of same-sex marriages. We can't file a joint tax return, and we're not eligible for bene-fits—not in any state—like spousal social security. My partner receives health benefits from her [employer], but I'm not eligible for any benefits as a spouse. Those are the issues we're trying to address. We have orga-nized, but finding the time and energy is another thing.*

I've [also] been struggling with certain issues in therapy. I think there's a certain element of perfectionism in Jewish people. We're doers. We al-ways have to strive for better and we have big hearts. We want to feed everyone, but the kitchen's not big enough. There's some sort of drive, *maybe from our immigrant background. The gist of it is to be hard on yourself and go past the standards, and past and past and past. It's never good enough.*

We've been asked by gays and straight friends both, if having a child together is visiting a hardship on [the child]. I tend to be optimistic about the changes in society and I don't see it as a problem. There's enough gays raising children, having them or adopting them, and in five years all these kids will be in kindergarten and it'll be easier.

The struggles we have are the struggles of straight couples. I want to please her so I give up, oftentimes, things for myself, and that's a deep struggle, putting her before me. What about me? We have to make money, we have to survive. Get a full-time job I'm miserable in, or take time for myself?

For me, the balancing act is an ongoing struggle. Not only with me and my partner but, even at age thirty-five, my mother's approval still means a lot to me. I've struggled to be an intellectual success. She was valedictorian, she worked for NASA. And my siblings are high achievers. I'm not. I'm not a fast-track person.

My partner and I, we're committed for life. Absolutely.

While homosexual unions are still not recognized as legal entities except in Vermont, we see dissident clergy blessing those unions even in the Catholic Church, an action forbidden by Rome. Rev. James Callan, for example, blesses same-sex marriages and allows women a prominent role at the altar. This caused his suspension in 1999. But the times they are a-changing.

According to the *New York Times,* new clinics have emerged that, like the Michael Callen–Audre Lorde Community Health Center in New York, are supportive of gay patients. Similar centers have opened in such large cities as Boston, San Francisco, and Los Angeles. And the Institute of Medicine, a division of the National Academy of Science, has urged the federal government to support studies to test myths about sexually transmitted diseases, breast cancer, drugs, and alcoholism among gays.

Tracy's struggles about issues of Jewish perfectionism, about raising a child Jewish when your partner is not Jewish, and about financial survival are the struggles of straight couples, too. However, *lesbian rights* are her political focus. Clearly, trying to keep sexual secrets interferes with medical care and psychological well-being, an extraheavy burden.

When she smiles, I see her crow's-feet, and I think, Too young to fight all those battles. Too hard to juggle all those issues. For Tracy, the struggle to balance work and love is compounded by her sexual orientation.

Three political women. Each with her own agenda. For Amy, gun control and civil rights issues. For Rona, women's empowerment and the end of the death penalty. For Tracy, gay rights. These political women insist on making a difference.

In the next chapter, you'll meet three women who are *professional volunteers*. Their work is unpaid. Some people accuse them of being social climbers, dilettantes, and show-offs. Because they are not in the workplace and earn not a penny, they can be the target of jealousy, their efforts undervalued.

5

PROFESSIONAL

VOLUNTEERS

ELINOR

RHODA

SHARON

A belief in social justice has always been an integral part of being Jewish. To be a good Jew requires more than just piety, observances, and rituals. Jews are enjoined to be charitable and do good deeds. We honor the tradition called *tzedakka*.

As Americans, we like to say, "Put your money where your mouth is." So we write checks, fund foundations, and support causes. We even donate used cars, clothing, and furniture. Some claim that immigrant Jews invented recycling because nothing was permitted to go to waste. I remember my grandmother Rachel at her sewing machine. She made us beautiful cloth dolls from scraps of leftover material, embroidering dark eyelashes and cherry lips.

We also emphasize that reaching out to non-Jews as well as Jews, is required. As a result, Jewish philanthropic organizations support colleges, civil rights, women's issues, politics, medical research, and the arts. On the local level, we get involved in our communities, working for PTA, Little League, and Fourth of July celebrations. And when a tragedy strikes someone in our neighborhood, we join together as Americans to raise money for the families involved. *Tzedakka.*

"The 1990 National Jewish Population Study" suggests that 56 percent of American Jews contribute to Jewish causes. Researchers say that contributing to *Jewish* causes is related to the intensity of our Jewish identification. Religious Jews, fearing assimilation, may fund organizations that promote Jewish identity, while secular Jews may respond to a crisis in Israel. Whatever the reasons, signing up for Jewish committees goes back to the *pishka,* the little box that beckoned you to drop in a few coins for the less fortunate. My mother rolled bandages for the Red Cross. She also earned plaques from Hadassah and ORT, the Organization for Rehabilitation through Training. For Jewish women, membership in service organizations offered satisfaction and pride. Some volunteers learned leadership skills as well.

However, as Americans work harder and the work week expands, many predict the death of volunteerism. We may continue to cut a check to the United Jewish Appeal, but how many of us still have *time* to give? As dual-career families become the model, will volunteer work be fazed out of our lives?

In Sylvia Barack Fishman's book *A Breath Of Life: Feminism in the American Jewish Community*, she traces the changes in volunteerism. In the 1960s, like my mother, "Most American Jewish women did not work after marriage unless there was dire financial need." Their husbands would be embarrassed. However, volunteering for ORT and Hadassah provided an "outlet for [their] intellectual, organizational, and social energies." Highly educated women wanted to do something with their brains and volunteering was culturally approved.

Today, however, most women are employed and eager to bring home a paycheck. Economic realities have pushed Jewish women into the marketplace; changes in attitude, feminism, and higher education have spurred them on. Nevertheless, to a nucleus of professional volunteers, their work is truly their life. Despite the fact that they are still excluded from executive positions in some Jewish organizations, many have risen to leadership roles and are highly visible in the Jewish press. They deserve our applause.

In this chapter, three professional volunteers tell us why they do it. They earn not a penny, but they devote their lives to Jewish causes. Are they a dying breed, an anachronism? Are they the dinosaurs of the new millennium of work, work, work for money, money, money?

Elinor

ELINOR, 61, is a born and bred southern lady. Her pastel blue knit suit with its gleaming gold buttons is set off by a silk print scarf and a gold lapel pin. With her dark eyes shining, there is something soft and sweet about her, a woman dipped in southern charm. Her voice is well modulated, her gestures feminine, and her speech melodic.

But make no mistake. This is a steel butterfly with an intelligence that gives weight to her every word. Her aura of southern gentility is only the patina of a woman of keen sensibilities and fierce commitments.

Born in Memphis, where she still lives, she is married to a former newspaperman turned attorney and has three grown children.

"I've always told my girls there are some things I do for love and some things I do for money. My volunteer work I do out of love. But I taught Sunday school for money and even if I gave it back, I was paid."

She explains that Memphis, a city close to a million people, is considered the Deep South, a region which also includes the area of Arkansas and Mississippi around the Mississippi Delta.

"People like to say the Delta begins in the lobby of the Peabody Hotel in Memphis."

Elinor is a full-time professional volunteer. As president of the Brandeis University National Women's Committee, she travels to conferences and meetings across the country.

I WAS BROUGHT up in a Reform home, but I recall wonderful Pass-over seders at my Orthodox grandparents' home. In the South, Reform was truly Ultra-Reform, very little Hebrew and we worked and drove on Saturdays. But my mother lit candles on Friday night, and no bread on Passover.

My mother, and what she did, influenced my decision to do what I did.

She was a working woman, very bright, at a time when women didn't work. Working was all she knew. And she began a business with my father. It was the first infant and children's furniture store in the South, around 1940, and then she expanded that to include children's clothing.

Well, I very much resented that she wasn't home like all the other mothers. I didn't come home to an empty house, no, because in the South many people, not necessarily wealthy, had cooks and house-keepers. I grew up with a housekeeper and we had a wonderful friend-ship because that's who was home. [But] I resented it; I did. And I said, "If I don't have to work when I get married and have children, I won't! I'll stay home and bake cookies and go to PTA and Brownie meetings." And I did!

Volunteer work started for me when I was in high school. Even in my little Jewish sorority, you had to put in charity hours, maybe at a veteran hospital or a community thing. My mother was too busy, but I felt an ob-ligation. We grew up in a time that you did things for other people; that was the message in those days.

Even when my husband and I were first married and stationed in Nu-remberg, Germany, for a year, I was a Gray Lady, a volunteer in the army hospital. And when we came back to live in Columbus, Georgia, where my husband worked on a newspaper, I began working for my tem-ple Sisterhood. I think charity was a part of our Jewish tradition, yes; it certainly was. We were taught that not only should you give money, but also some of yourself: tzedakka.

My husband was from a small town in Alabama, La Fayette, the only Jewish family in the county. And the only person who could teach him Hebrew for his bar mitzvah was the Methodist minister. But we were Jews with Jewish values based on ethics. And later when we went back to Memphis when my husband went to law school, I taught Sunday school and developed a reading readiness curriculum for kindergarten and first grade, teaching the aleph bet.

I had two years of college, but I quit because in the fifties the message was, girls weren't supposed to be smart or they weren't desirable. Pretty was a lot more important. I wanted to get married and raise a family. I was working part time for twenty dollars a week, but I was never career oriented. I was totally content to be home. I taught myself to sew and cook—my mother couldn't boil water—and I loved it.

I remember I would beg my mother, "Play with me," play with me, and she'd say, "In a minute." She was working on something for the business. Well, I played with my children. We made paper dolls, we played cards and board games and I enjoyed every minute of it. I had minimal household help, two days a week, but I felt that's what a woman's priority should be. That to raise wonderful children was a tremendous accomplishment.

And in the scheme of things, we now have wonderful children. In fact, they fulfill every statistic. Our oldest is a single mom doing computer programming and raising a seven-year-old in Ashland, Oregon. Our middle one, in Clearwater, Florida, did not complete college. She's married and works out of her home so she can be with her two children. Our youngest is single, an editor in New York City. We were lucky. Our children survived the seventies and didn't stray too far. We really loved them, they felt that, and it transcended the peer pressure.

As a professional volunteer, I've been involved in the intensive aspects of volunteerism for thirty years. In Memphis I joined a chapter of the Brandeis University National Women's Committee, the organization that raises money for the Brandeis Library. My friend was president and I felt Brandeis was special, different, an enrichment in my life. There were study groups and one of our big fundraisers was a used book sale, and I loved books. I became involved locally, then regionally, and then nationally. I stayed with it and they became interested in me. The friends I've made across the country are part of the reward.

I think every kind of work has to have rewards. Work in the home has family rewards. Work outside the home has money. And sometimes people put up with a lot in the workplace because they need the money. For volunteers, the rewards are the people. Aside from doing good things and the feeling you're making a difference, I think if you ask volunteers in Jewish organizations, they'd say the rewards are the personal relationships, that's what keeps them involved: women of similar interests and values.

For me, that we are connected to a prestigious university was very appealing because I didn't have a college degree. Ultimately, I went back to school and in 1993 I got my bachelor's degree. It took me seven years part time, and this validated everything I was doing; I was growing in leadership skills.

Right now, I'm flying all over the country and my husband is so supportive. I never would have taken this position without checking with family first. It's been an amazing opportunity, giving me a feeling of achievement. I have always said I was fortunate to have the option not to work. To me, that is the ultimate women's liberation.

At home, I put in four to six hours a day on the phone and writing letters. And I come to Brandeis in Waltham, Massachusetts, one week out of every month. Our office has a staff of fourteen. I have an executive director [who] is my counterpart and we consult regularly. But I am the link to 105 chapters throughout the country. Every year there are regional conferences and this year I attended five within five weeks, traveling from Los Angeles to Williamsburg, Virginia; to West Palm Beach; to Detroit; and to Boston—going home in between to unpack, do laundry, and repack, and to say hello to my husband. And that's been intense.

Unfortunately, today volunteerism is decreasing because women are working, and they simply can't juggle work and children and volunteering. Also, there's no longer the same sense of obligation. Today life is different from the immigrant experience. Not even knowing someone who has to do without, there's not the same sense of compassion.

We hear about the "me generation," the family that has to have two incomes to take trips and drive large cars and buy expensive toys. In the South, which has always been conservative, people who have money do not flaunt it. But for some Jewish women, there's the feeling of materialism, the clothes and the jewelry and the status.

It is harder and harder to get volunteers. Time has become a commodity as valuable as money, so we have to look for ways to attract women. The reality is to make them think there's something in it for them. Because the status women once got through volunteering, they now get through work.

But I see a trend back, to look at life the way I did. [To say] maybe I do want to spend those years at home with my children. I observe that women are seeking ways to work from home, realizing they don't have to be making money to do something worthwhile.

In the seventies, women wanted to work, staying home was not worthwhile. So they opened little boutiques or went back to school. In the eighties, money was the only important reward. Now, even among men—I see doctors who are changing what they do. The glamor of the working woman has faded. The excitement of dressing up in the power suit and going to a meeting—today, it's different.

Some young women will choose to stay home and [do] volunteer work. But Jews are oriented to giving their kids the best education. That could mean private schools and expensive colleges. It takes a lot of money to give them those advantages.

The stresses of the new millennium are enormous.

Elinor observes that *time* has become more important than money. We see family restaurants packed, we see take-out foods and convenience items chosen without hesitation. With women juggling jobs and families, services that save time are necessary in a day that needs to be thirty hours long.

What will this mean for volunteerism?

Where once a woman's position on a Jewish committee established her visibility, identity, and status in the community, today this is earned from the workplace, which provides the additional benefits of salary, health insurance, the status of earning money outside the home.

Is Elinor's view, that women will turn back to *her* choice and stay home, a likely scenario? Will Jewish organizations find ways to attract a new breed of volunteers? Or will the concept of *tzedakka* reinvent itself in ways we cannot imagine?

Rhoda

RHODA, 69, is a blue-eyed blond and an avid gardener. We sip coffee in the sunny breakfast room of her gracious home, overlooking a spectacular view of the New York skyline.

A prominent New Jersey philanthropist married to a two-star United States Air Force general, she gives back every cent her business earns and travels widely to assess the needs of Jewish communities from Israel to Cuba.

Wearing khaki pants and a sweater, no jewelry, and a swipe of lipstick, she looks more like a preppie than the "lady of the house." Devoted for years to Jewish causes, Rhoda had no Jewish upbringing whatsoever. "We had Christmas dinners, Passover dinners, and Easter dinners. It was all related to the stomach."

Like many Jewish families in Newark's Weequahic section, her brother received private tutoring for his bar mitzvah, plus a lavish party at the Clinton Manor. "I had nothing, zilch, zero. We didn't even belong to a temple."

Still, she always felt Jewish. Her partner in the flower business is her girlfriend from first grade. "She invited me to High Holidays at B'nai Abraham. That was the extent of it."

A graduate of George Washington University with a degree in zoology, she married at twenty and traveled with her husband from 1950 to 1954. Her first child was born in England.

In 1961, she launched her flower business.

WE CREATED HUGE *trees and ming bowls, all individual projects, all word of mouth. We built it up from our kitchen tables into a thriving, respected business. I didn't have to work, my husband had a very successful insurance business; but he encouraged me. He was gone two months of the year for the air force. I was alone with the kids, so I took them along and made them interested in my work. And once they were in school, we expanded into the corporate world. We'd create a garden in an office building. My earnings went into charities 100 percent.*

At sixty, my husband retired from the United States Air Force as a two-star general. From his class at West Point, I know only three or four Jewish generals, but they don't live as Jews. And he stepped into the world of Jewish philanthropy on a major *scale and devoted himself to UJA [United Jewish Appeal]. He has meetings Monday through Thursday evenings; we have dinner together on Friday.*

How did [our philanthropy] come about? It goes back to 1954 in England, when my first child was born and I was diagnosed with cancer of the thyroid. After the surgery, I had an epiphany. I made my pact with God. If I could live to raise this child, who was six weeks old, I promised myself and my Creator I would be the best person I knew how to be. I try never to let that bargain escape from me.

Our lives have been so blessed. We are both absorbed and involved, and I love what I'm doing, [though] my business is now down to a trickle.

We've traveled all over the world for Jewish causes. Israel ten, fifteen times; Hungary; Ukraine; Poland; Paris; Cuba, where it's two cents for a loaf of bread, earning eighteen dollars a month. A lot are choosing to be Jews and going through conversion with only the help of itinerant rabbis from Argentina and New York.

When one sees the suffering in the world and you come home, you say, "How can this be? What can I do to make a difference?"

I do a lot of fundraising for the women's division of UJA, I'm vice president and advisor to Outreach. We're trying to broaden the base, to reach women under forty who have never been involved in the Jewish community. I've met some marvelous young women; it's heartening. They've cho-

sen [to] stay home—most are lucky to be financially able—and they bring their kids with them. Some are employed part time and they're balancing work and family and volunteering.

What are the traits required to be a professional volunteer? Where does [my passion] come from? The reinforcement is the travel. You see things firsthand. When I talk to people about what they should be doing, it's easy because I have those memories in my head which never leave me. And I believe firmly in Tikkun olam—"to save the world." And clal Israel—"we're all Jews," brothers and sisters. It never leaves my psyche, it's deeply ingrained.

I keep a diary when I travel, I take pictures, and I show them at meetings and I talk about the people I've met. A photojournalist told us to visit people in the Ukraine. [One man] there told us the story of his life, [how he] hid in a public toilet to escape and now takes care of his mentally ill wife. So when I see these people, it's emblazoned in my heart and it's so easy to speak with passion. I speak from the heart. I was nervous at first, but after fifteen years, it's easy.

What part is frustrating? We have 121,000 Jews in our community and I see less and less *people are giving* more and more. Which means people are slipping through the cracks, disinterested, totally assimilated. They know they're Jewish, but it doesn't mean a lot. They're not interested in joining the crusade to save Jews. I find it very disheartening, very disturbing.

Even with women working, what you want to make time for, you make time for. If you want to become involved, even with your dollars, it's not hard to do. But I find a lot of resistance: "How dare you call me on a Sunday morning!" A lot of self-involvement today. If they knew how lucky they were, they'd stand up and say "I'll do anything."

Our Israel Program Center [IPC] offers [young people] a free trip to Israel. They send us a shilach (male) or shilhah (female) as a messenger from Israel. We subsidize these trips with the hope that the [young] will become observant and more Jewish and ultimately make aliya. Edgar Bronfman of Seagram's has put millions into a [similar] project called Birthright.

With women working for money, there's a loss of volunteers. I recently went on a trip we call a mini-mission. Through Outreach, we get women on a bus to visit our own Jewish community, not the Ukraine or Cuba, so they see there are needs to be met right here at home. They see [programs] to help Jews become citizens, learn English, use a computer, get a job, and help the disabled. We expose them to geriatric centers and Jewish Family Services.

The difficult part is to get the women to go. Buses leave at four different times so they can be home for their kids. When you're dealing with young women, you're battling time.

We have to know we're here to save the world, to be a light unto the world. Being Jewish [is] a formidable task, we have to give all our energies.

Jews have always been on the forefront of education. There are more Jewish Nobelists than any other people; Jews are in the headlines for medicine and literature.

I've alway felt lucky to be a Jewish woman. I know how to balance my life, how to use my thoughts and intelligence to lead me. I know how to put myself aside. I find being Jewish and a professional volunteer is very gratifying.

Rhoda speaks of a sense of mission and a crusade to save the world and the Jews. Her level of dedication is uncommon.

What she bemoans are the *assimilated Jews* for whom being Jewish doesn't mean a lot and *working women* who have no time for volunteer work. Can these Jews be retrieved? Can Jews be reimpassioned, rededicated, and reclaimed? Are mini-missions and free trips to Israel, Outreach and IPC, viable solutions?

Sharon

SHARON, 81, is the mother of three daughters, grandmother of five, step-grandmother of two, and great-grandmother of three. "I'll talk to you from fifty years of volunteering," she promises me on the phone.

She pulls into the hotel parking lot waving energetically. She sits down in front of the tape recorder, unfolds her notes, and flicks a crumb off her smart pastel pantsuit. It is 8:15 A.M.

Widowed at fifty-three and a Floridian for twelve years, she recalls her parents' blue box hanging on the back of the pantry door for trees in Palestine. "We were raised to believe the world has to be a better place because you lived in it."

A graduate of Mount Sinai School of Nursing, she worked in the emergency room and was head nurse; but once she married in the 1940s, being a mother became her full-time job. "Hadassah was the fourth child at our table every night."

When her youngest was in high school she went back to work. "Part time, because my husband had a custom milinery shop and he wanted me to be available to help him in the store."

Two months after he died, she returned to work. "I *had* to, there wasn't enough to take me past six months." But she never stopped volunteering. Active in PTA, League of Women Voters, and Mother's March for Mental Health, she started the first child guidance clinic in Essex County, New Jersey. She also served as chapter president of Hadassah, the Women's Zionist Organization of America, whose more than three-hundred-thousand members work in large measure to ensure Jewish continuity and strengthen American Jews' partnership with Israel.

I BECAME INVOLVED in interfaith work when my children were very small, and [I] started the first Human Relations Council because community service, whether it was Jewish or not, was important to me. Today's young women who don't volunteer, I feel sorry for them. Because a very strong part of fulfilling your soul, your spirit, is giving. Maimonides said the highest form of giving is when neither the donor nor the recipient knows each other.

Something is lost today: the meaning of the blue box. Children are not raised to give, they're raised to get. I see it all around me. They want goods rather than good feelings, [they're] accumulating things rather than doing things for others. Having a cause is very important, not clothes or cars or tennis bracelets. But it's difficult to go against the trend.

I've been to Israel twice and, God willing, I'm going again next year. As a past chapter president of Hadassah, it was heartwarming to see the fruits of my labors all those years. The huge medical center with Arab mothers holding their babies, that gave me a special feeling. I feel very strongly children should learn about giving, that tzedakka is the corner-stone of being a fulfilled human being.

I also work hard as a professional volunteer for non-Jewish organiza-tions. Racial relations is our number one problem today. I started an interfaith coalition with non-Jews and formed the Committee for Social Justice in my Reform temple. I also started an annual children's concert for many denominations—black, white, brown, Hindu, Buddhist, Jew-ish. We're a very diverse group and we had over a thousand people hear them sing. It was standing room only! Eleven different denominations represented. My dream is Beethoven's Ninth Symphony with all the chil-dren singing together the last chorus.

For me, Jews must get all people to work together and it's not easy. Al-most impossible to get Christian fundamentalists. It's very slow; we have to work constantly, like the pioneers who went to Palestine to work the land before it was Israel. We have to reach out to others, and I see people in the non-Jewish community who are truly devoted to one humanity. Without it, our children have no future.

I'm a life member of Hadassah, I'm on the Nurses' Council and I lec-ture on osteoporosis and breast examination. I was born a feminist! I was always emancipated and when I weakened, my husband got behind me and pushed. He edited my speeches and was right there with me. And when he got beef stew—dinner in one plate—he'd ask me, "Which meet-ing are you going to?"

At Hadassah we're taught Judaism is a way of life. When you educate a man, you educate an individual. When you educate a woman, you edu-cate the family. As a volunteer, you get no pay for what you're doing. Don't expect instant gratification, don't have unrealistic expectations. Whatever the level of giving is, just accept and say thank you.

Sharon's commitment to Hadassah and race relations is part of her Judaism. She is infused with the concept of giving and making the world a better place.

Is that what fuels professional volunteers?

Surely, these three women—Elinor, Rhoda, and Sharon—have demonstrated their motivation. Earning not a penny for their efforts, they are dedicated to *tikkun olam.* They speak of causes and missions, of feeding their souls.

Reaching out to others, *non-*Jews as well as Jews, was recently celebrated by the Reform movement, noting two decades of *keruv,* Hebrew for "bringing closer" and welcoming the stranger. Is all this lost on young working women?

Elinor, Rhoda, and Sharon appear despondent on this issue, noting that fewer volunteers are available and willing to give their time. With *time* at a premium in dual-career families, with single moms working and raising kids, it's hard to fault these overburdened women. Even if they agree that there is much to be gained from volunteering—close friendships, a sense of satisfaction, skills, and self-confidence—how can they fit it into their overscheduled days?

Can we look to seniors who have retired from the workforce? The *Newark Star Ledger* reports that Americans fifty-five and over are the most likely group to pursue volunteer work, with 34 percent giving more than five hours a week. Perhaps retirement among Jewish working women may add to the rolls of volunteers.

I've witnessed this myself: retired women who have returned to volunteer work with spirit and energy. They are pleased to give back, to be busy, to enrich the lives of others. Their days are fuller because they're needed.

Perhaps the picture is not so bleak.

The *Nonprofit Almanac 1996–1997* reported more than one hundred million Americans are working to make their communities a better place to live. Many volunteers report that they get back more than they give.

Perhaps the tide is turning. Some companies, concerned about the burnout of their employees and an attrition rate of 20 percent, are limiting the workload to a forty-hour week, suggesting employees build *a life beyond work*. In the Silicon Valley where a sixteen-hour day is the norm, a get-a-life counselor may coach the worker on the joys of children and sunshine. Medical claims go down and errors decrease, along with depression, fatigue, and confusion. Perhaps we will move back to a more realistic workload and "getting a life" will return us to volunteering.

Jewish philanthropy is not limited to women over sixty, or high-powered and high-profile leaders. Volunteers who set an example enrich their children's lives. What childern see, they do. Sharon remembers the blue box.

In the next chapter you'll meet three *married women with children*, trying to achieve a balance between work and love. Committed to their families and eager to do well at their jobs, they are constantly on the line: frustrated, overworked, and fatigued. Here's how they manage.

6

MARRIED WOMEN
WITH CHILDREN

NANCY

CINDY

NAOMI

Several years ago I had tea with Gloria Steinem and her Persian cat Magritte in her Upper East Side apartment. We talked about feminism and the challenges facing contemporary working women. Steinem believes that feminism doesn't kick in until a woman is thirty or forty, *when she responds to her own feelings.*

"What happens is you discover *you're* not crazy, it's the *system* that's crazy!"

True. Many working women are struggling with an intolerable system that taxes their sanity and their health. The culture tells them they are bad mothers if they *don't* go to the school play, and bad employees if they *do* go and take time off from work.

In this chapter you'll hear three married women with children tell us how they tried to keep their balance and not go crazy in workplaces whose policies often increase the pressures on family life.

Nancy

NANCY wept as she told me about her four-year-old's sudden life-threatening illness. How it affected her husband, her parents, her older son, and herself. How do you keep going to work when you're told your child might die?

She is wearing shorts and a camp shirt, sneakers, and a dab of lip gloss. She has big dark eyes and tons of curly black hair. We talk over coffee in the hotel where I'm staying.

NANCY, 44, got married at 25 and gave up a job she loved at Yerkes Primate Research Center in Atlanta, Georgia, to move to Manhattan, where her husband worked on Wall Street. With an undergraduate degree in biology and a master's in teaching, she taught for a year, but left the job to have a child. She was 31 and her husband was doing well, so they decided to move to Florida where her sister lived. Her second son was born there and she stayed home with the kids and did some tutoring.

"My husband was the breadwinner. I tutored in the evenings or weekends. The children came first."

But seven years ago, things changed. Her husband's job was not going well; he was doing consulting. When a teaching job came up at a Jewish day school, she took it. They needed the health insurance. She also took her second grader out of public school and enrolled him in her school.

"It was nice, we all drove together and came home together, a seven-minute ride."

She taught science, sixth to eighth grade; she wrote the curriculum; and she watched the department grow.

"It was the right timing and I became the senior person."

Nancy is now the department chair, developing her own environmental courses and redefining fifth to ninth grade science.

However, in between, tragedy struck.

FIVE YEARS AGO, *my four-year-old got sick. A malignant brain tumor. We didn't know if he would survive and we brought him home like an infant. He lost physical ability, he couldn't walk, he had to learn how to sit up. The prognosis was long term and we weren't given stats about remission rates. One minute he was a healthy kid running around. It came out of the blue. It was the first year I was teaching and the health insurance was all on me. Thank God I had it.*

Because I *had the health insurance, my husband had to give up his job to take care of* him. *At this point my parents had moved here. If not for them, we would* not *have survived.*

For the first six weeks, my husband took him every morning for treatments and my parents watched him every afternoon. We didn't know if he'd live. I *still perceive it as* my child could die. *I don't plan things in advance; it's one day at a time.*

The following year we hired someone to come in every day. Once a month he had to be in the hospital in Miami for the weekend, and my sister and parents took care of our older boy. It put things in perspective. Prior to his illness and our money difficulties we were . . . well, it changed our priorities.

In the second year we had a physical therapist. She worked with him on handwriting and swimming. He's an upbeat kid and we're now five years out. He's going to be nine and he's come very far. But he still can't run or jump.

The tumor was removed, but the surgeon would not guarantee 100 percent. He had to do radiation and chemo and he's left with a ripple effect—a lot of learning disabilities. He has a hard time processing information, difficulty learning to read. He's never going to memorize math and multiplication tables. He was a very bright kid when all of this happened.

Through it all I *continued to work.* I *had to,* I *couldn't quit, no one else would give us health insurance. During the day, the teaching kept me focused on the job; it was my saving grace. And being a Jewish woman, it was engrained in me to have standards, to take pride in what you do.*

How did I balance it all? How did I do it?

I'd go to work, come home in late afternoon, and make dinner for everyone. And when the kids went to bed, I'd go back and do my school-work. Teaching allows you to take care of their needs. That's how I managed, I got back to [being] mommy.

My husband and I divided the tasks. We were both working, we both did the wash. He picked the kids up, he took them to the doctor, he was the one. The only thing that remained [for me] was dinner and cleaning up.

I could not have survived those years without my parents. I don't know if they realize how much they helped us. Without a family . . . no one else has the same interest in your health and well-being. My mother was phenomenal.

And we're tighter with our kids now. It's the four of us. We've [even] been to Disneyland. You don't notice his physical disability until he tries to keep up.

Taking it day by day is what got us through. We didn't dwell on the sickness or [cry], "Why me?" and "Woe is me." My husband would say, "Just move on"; he's the upbeat one. [But] if someone said, "You have a choice: your marriage falls apart or your child [gets] sick," I'd say, "The marriage." The bond between mother and child is the strongest; you can't replace your child. My priorities are his physical needs, it all centers around him. Once our older boy asked me, "When he's better, will the attention be divided?"

Today my husband is with a brokerage house, a nine-to-five job. And we do everything together, we go out as a family. I don't go out with girl-friends, I'd feel guilty. I get together with my core group of friends every two months, but I don't call friends during the week and sit on the phone. And I don't go out after work. I'm tired at the end of my day and sometimes I lose patience at home.

At work, the administration was very attentive, very sensitive. When my son first got sick, they'd cover my classes, they let me take off and get out. They gave our older son a support system and [when he asked] they taught him a prayer for his sick brother. It gave him a strong Jewish identity.

I saw people do care about each other. The Jewish community is an ex-tended family. The school raised money and did tzedakka *for his therapy and rehabilitation. Florida [can be] a hard state, and all of a sudden we saw we had a* family *when the crisis came. It came from the Jewish com-munity. Not just the school. [It was] the whole campus of South Palm Beach Jewish Federation. Through their monetary support and the insu-rance, we got through.*

The balancing act I had to do was I had to keep focused and not be consumed. Having work was a help. It kept a normalcy and it gave me a chance to have something else, not dwelling on why, why, why. Work was the saving grace for my mental health. But my husband was the last per-son to get the attention, and that's not fair.

Suppose Nancy worked for IBM or Macy's? Would that employer have given her anything near the support she received from her actual em-ployer? Fortunately, she worked for a Jewish day school and the Jewish community rallied around her, reacting swiftly and generously. That, however, is rare in a workplace which computes compassion in bottom-line dollars.

Nancy also talked about her parents' contribution, a theme you hear often in Jewish families. In contrast to media images of overbearing, controlling Jewish mothers, Nancy shows us the loving support her mother provided, the tight bond between adult women and their moth-ers. Also, that tenderest of bonds between grandparents and their grandchildren.

Gloria Steinem, now past sixty-five, was asked by *Modern Maturity Magazine* about her life if she had married and had children. She re-plied, "I'm not sure I would have been strong enough to have children, to live that life, and to come out the other end with an identity of my own. . . . I could not give birth to both myself and someone else. It was a choice."

Nancy chose to have children and chose to work. Facing the pos-sible death of her child, she chose to be strong.

Sylvia Barack Fishman, author of *A Breath Of Life*, states, "Today the majority of Jewish women expect to be employed for pay throughout their lives, including during their children's preschool years."

Thirty years ago, American women had little faith in their ability to support themselves. Today, they receive 60 percent of the nation's college degrees and make up nearly half the students in medical and law schools. Among two-income families, nearly a quarter of the wives out-earn their husbands. These women have chosen to have both a family and a worklife.

Cindy

CINDY, 43, is a pretty Floridian wearing white shorts and sneakers. She's vivacious, with a husky Lauren Bacall voice, and she exudes high energy. But there's pain buried in her dark eyes.

A full-time marketer in a dual-career family, Cindy made another kind of choice. She decided to pick up stakes and move to Florida. Why? "So my child would know his grandmother."

With a B.A. in psychology and an M.A. in early childhood development, Cindy taught for seven years, then went into copier sales. "I made four times more money! Rose through the ranks to sales manager, trainer, national sales trainer, and recruitment development."

She and her second husband were both traveling; he was District Manager for the same company. Her earlier marriage had ended in divorce at twenty-four. Each time she married non-Jews.

"I'm Jewish by culture, not religion, and my husband is a completely lapsed Catholic."

Remarried at thirty-six to a man with two teenagers, she and her husband were fast-track careerists. So when he wanted to move to Texas, she extracted a bargain. "*You* get what you want and *I get to have a baby*. That was the trade-off."

She thought she'd hire a nanny and go on with her life.

BUT ONCE I *held my son, I knew I couldn't go back. I also knew it would drive me nuts to stay home. We didn't need two incomes in Dallas, so I took a family leave for four months and stayed home.*

It was total shock! I had post-partum depression, I couldn't even get dressed. It was killing me. So I figured okay, I'll be mommy-track and leave at five. I interviewed sixty people and I found exceptional daycare for my son.

The problem was my being dependent—that was the depresssion. Your identity's gone, you don't know who you are. And with older mothers, it's "Wait a minute. Wow! What did I get myself into?" Your mind isn't the same. I was in control before he was born and I never would be in control again.

After the four months' leave, I returned to work.

What's the working mother's big secret? It's no big deal. When you work full time, you have to be organized. Errands get done over lunch hour; I'd flit to five different places. At my desk I had respect, and daycare provided a far better [person] than I could have been as a full-time mom. She was patient and laid back. I had an understanding boss. Occasionally he and I hit the bar at four o'clock; he was not demanding.

I picked up my son, got home at six, and I never cooked a meal that took more than fifteen minutes. Stir fry or broil. When my husband walked in at six-thirty, I put my son in the highchair and we had dinner together.

We shared everything. We were equal partners. I was providing half the income, he was providing half the childcare and half the chores. The baby was asleep by eight-fifteen and the rest of the evening was our time.

I came to realize that there's a lot of things no longer in my control. There's this other person who needs to eat or sleep, and whatever I want to do goes out the window; that's part of mothering. You're no longer free and that becomes okay. You work it out in stages.

I had it all, I did. I was working full time. An excellent boss. Daycare. My husband sharing the parenting. I had it all.

And then my mother got ill, very ill. And suddenly it's not just your kid, it's your parent. The forties are the crunch years. And I made some very wrong choices.

I left an ideal situation to go to my mother. She had been trying for years to get me to Florida. We are unnaturally close, maybe even un-healthfully close. My mother and I are enmeshed. If someone asked me, who was more important to me, my husband or my mother, it would have been my mother.

It may be unique to Jewish and Italian families—there's something about the mother-daughter thing. I desperately wanted to bring her grandson home to her. I saw myself raising my son with my mother, even before she became ill. We'd come down to visit three times a year and I was hell-bent to get us there because the fantasy was: My mother's here! We'll move to Florida and everything will be hunky-dory.

I found my husband a job here, a six-figure job. I'd get to pal around with my mom. Be a full-time mom. What a concept! My mother is here, my aunt, my grandmother; this is my nuclear family, my birth family.

Having a child—well, with Jewish women—it doesn't matter what went on before. Because I wanted my son to grow up with his grand-mother. It was almost primal. I had to go home and it didn't matter that "home" was with my husband. I'm just learning that now.

I did my mother's bidding, I was a good daughter, I was on this earth to make sure she was happy. I see it in many Jewish families. The expec-tations of non-Jews are they expect the kids to grow up and lead their own lives. My family expected me to come home! "Bring me my grand-child."

Jewish and Italian and Cuban daughters are bonded to their mothers and there's a very subtle level of expectation. Daughters are supposed to be there for their mothers. I wanted to please my mother and I wanted my son to have his grandmother. All I wanted to do was lay my son in my grandmother's arms. I wanted that close circle.

My husband respected my need for this. So we moved.

What happened? He got the six-figure job. I was the stay-at-home mom. And my mother got very ill. One month after we arrived, she was diagnosed with lung cancer. She fought it for a year and she died on August thirteen. On August fifteen, my husband was let go. That was about as intense as it gets.

I had to go back to work. I took a nine-thirty to two-thirty job; I constructed my life around my son. And now all the guilt kicked in. I went from "I can't be a full-time mom," to "I can't go back to a full-time job." And the job my husband gave up to come down here, he'll never get that satisfaction back. And when my husband [isn't] happy, no one's happy.

We are still struggling with financial problems. In my forties, I'm having to examine what's important. My sister is here now, with my son's only cousin. We hate Florida. We came here for my family and we can't go back to Texas.

Where am I now? I'm working through the grief and the anger and the loss of my mother. It was a huge sacrifice to move to Florida and I don't think she realized what we gave up. I went into a terrible tailspin. I miss her terribly. I'm in therapy trying to [understand.] Do I stay here so my son has a cousin? I don't know. We don't belong here, so it's a struggle. My son has no other family, only this cousin. I'm moving through a tunnel. It's priorities and passages.

The conflict between work and love—we had it all. Until we came to Florida. Jewish families—I don't see it in WASPs—[have] this clannishness, this pull, this tribalism. I hear it over and over. [Women saying], "After I had my baby, I wanted to be near my mother."

I believe women were meant to raise their children among other women, we're not meant to be alone. On a basic level I function on the premise that a woman must be a good mother before anything else. The Jewish mother thing is very real and passed on from mother to daughter. All I know is in my family that's how it was. Absolutely. Absolutely. I bought it!

Cindy raises some valid issues. What happens when a hell-bent careerist has a child and gives up work? Is she doomed to depression, doomed to lose her identity? Danielle Crittenden's book *What Our Mothers Didn't Tell Us* blames feminist advice, which she believes tells us that "the child should be the *first* spinning plate a woman drops, even if it's the most precious to her. She must *never* let go of the ones to do with work."

I don't read feminism that way, do you? Who said, "Sacrifice your kids to your job"? On the contrary, working moms, including career-ists, juggle competing demands to make sure their children are well taken care of. Cindy checked out *sixty* people before she chose her day-care arrangement.

For some lucky working moms, high-quality day care is located at their workplace. According to Burud & Associates, a work/life consult-ing firm, a study of 205 programs found that on-site childcare is "eight times more likely to meet the high standards set by the National Associ-ation for the Education of Young Children (NAEYC)."

Cindy was lucky. Her husband was an *equal* partner in parenting and household chores. This is uncommon. While women derive huge psychological benefits from working, they face another job when they come home. According to *Working Mother* magazine, the reality is that women still do more housework than men. While husbands may "pitch in," women wind up carrying the burden of responsibilities. Ac-cording to the *New York Times*, even those working part time (under thirty-five hours) are "shouldering more of the burden of minding the children or caring for elderly relatives," and often the part-time job adds up to a full-time job.

Indeed, the American workweek has expanded from 43.6 to 47.1 hours, not counting people who eat lunch at their computers. In four out of five marriages, both husband and wife go to work. To keep it all together we leave notes on the kitchen table, we use cell phones, beepers, and pagers. However, until the workplace becomes more family friendly with flex-time, telecomputing, shared jobs, and excel-lent daycare, working moms will continue to be physically and emo-tionally challenged.

Naomi

NAOMI, 42, an ophthalmologist, is married to a busy pediatrician. She has three children, 12, 10 and 3. Married in medical school at 23, she works two days a week and, like many in dual-career families, she is balancing work and love on a tight schedule, intricately arranged.

There is something quite charming about her: her confidence in who she is and how she got there, an insightful and cheerful look at her struggles, and a maturity in her vision. She has merry dark eyes and a light in her smile.

"I was the one who wanted the third, my husband was happy with two. He said, 'Okay, if you can handle it.' And once, when I complained, he reminded me."

Raised in an Orthodox home in Manhattan, her mom sent her to yeshiva at five, where she remained until eighth grade. From there she went on to a public high school.

"We didn't drive on the sabbath, so I walked to the winter concert. And no phones calls on the sabbath. But we did watch television."

A lot changed when she married her husband—a union not endorsed by her mom. Why? Because he was a Reform Jew.

TO MY MOTHER *he was Gentile and she tried to break it up. She said if we didn't get married in an Orthodox ceremony, she wouldn't make the wedding. He was twenty-five, a medical student, a lovely man, but to her it was like an intermarriage.*

I told him—like a prenuptial agreement—my only stipulation was I wanted to send our future children to a Jewish day school; was he willing? I felt solid, I mean I knew my values. We [made] an oral agreement and I knew he'd honor it. That was seven years before we even had children.

Today, I'm the one who deals directly with the school if I have issues.

He's the expert, the pediatrician. So Father is right, but Mother knows best.

The rest was an evolution. Because my husband is a very forceful man and he is not neutral about religion. He goes beyond that. He's actually anti-organized *religion. He finds it a little hocus-pocus, mumbo-jumbo; and our oldest, 12, knows his dad's feelings, he's pre–bar mitzvah. My husband believes in a higher power, but* not *organized religion, period. He doesn't go to temple, or he goes reluctantly if it's socially necessary, like a bar mitzvah. He'll be respectful, gracious. But it does nothing for him.*

We made compromises. *We're Conservative now.*

What enabled me to leave Orthodoxy was the narrow-mindedness, the feeling they *have the pipeline to God,* they *do it the right way. The Hassidim think the Orthodox are heathens and the Orthodox think we Conservatives are . . . Well, it depends on your perspective. Orthodox women may not be seated with men in the temple, they can't be rabbis or cantors. They're not counted in a minyan. They can't hold high offices. Their power is limited.*

But one of the things I remember from growing up is respect. One of the Ten Commandments is respecting your mother and father, a major issue with us. We tell our children, you must always be respectful.

At work, it's the Jewish ethics of being honorable and honest. I don't know that it's limited to Jewish. But that comes up in my field all the time. With the HMOs, there's this pressure to lie, the insurance companies are forcing you to lie. They want you to put down a category so they can bill the patient and collect.

I'm an ophthalmologist; a routine exam is often not covered. So patients want a diagnosis. And I say, "I can't, I really can't." If it's a routine exam, you can't manufacture an illness. Some doctors do it routinely. But I can't. It's a sense of integrity. There are doctors out there doing unnecessary surgery. Jewish doctors are doing it too. I mean it's from the Torah, the ethics you grew up with.

I'm part-time, which is two full days in the office. I did this specifically to raise my children myself. *Properly. Without nannies. For the past twelve years I have been their caretaker.*

The days that I work have always been backed up by family. My husband does one of my full workdays, my mother-in-law did the other for the first ten years, and three years ago my mom took over. The only way I turn over my children is if it's family. Because my children are the most valuable things in my life. My responsibility, and I'm going to give it my best.

I have friends who have good help. There are good people out there. So women should not feel guilty if they leave their children, absolutely not. As long as you find the person who shares your values. You interview them vigorously, absolutely.

The stress of ambitious dual-career families is it's the woman who is usually responsible for the care of the children, in spite of the fact that it's supposed to be an egalitarian society. Women have no time for themselves and they feel they're losing control over their children. Especially their teenagers and preteens. They're not home enough to be involved with their kids, so their kids find it easy to disrespect them, especially the ones traveling. I have found from experience, the more you're with the kids, the more you relate to them and the more you connect. If it's a full-time job and you have to travel, you're losing your family life.

I hear a lot from [my] patients. Professional women complain to me, they have panic attacks, they're very stressed out, they have no time. I say, "Well, maybe you can find part-time." And a couple have said, "I flexed from full time to part time and it's the best thing I ever did."

You have to give up the partnership-track mentality. I mentally said, "Well, I don't need to be a partner. I'll keep current and when I want to go [back] full time, I'll do it.

I've seen patients who have tried to have it all and it affects their health, physically and emotionally, and they wind up in the emergency room. They think they're having a heart attack. They're just overworked and stressed out.

Men don't have the dual responsibility of dealing with work and their children's schedules. We're the nurturers. Men can be nurturers too, but you have to be a certain kind of woman to relinquish the control in the household. [You can't] belittle the man if he doesn't do the job to your standards. The way I've been able to have my husband be Mr. Mom for twelve years is I put blinders on when I come home and the house looks like a tornado hit. I walk in exhausted at eight-thirty and all I ask is, "Is everybody okay? How are the kids?"

I nursed all three. It was embarrassing. At work, I'd occupy the bathroom for twenty minutes to pump and bring home the milk, and I tried to keep it as quiet as possible. I nursed my youngest daughter two years because she was born with a congenital heart disease and I was waiting for a surgical correction. They kept postponing it. But she's healthy now, she is terrific.

Knowing that you have to put yourself aside, it's hard. You need a backup, someone to talk to, a caretaker for a few hours so you can take care of yourself. That was real hard for me when she was sick. I either went to work or I was home, because I wouldn't allow her to be exposed to crowds. I didn't take her to a mall, I didn't take her to a supermarket, I didn't take her to the library.

I've been there, really stressed out, and I know you have to find what gives you the quickest dose of relaxation. Whether it's the treadmill or going shopping, you need a break. And if you need ancillary help, even if you can't afford it, you have to make yourself afford it. Otherwise you'll be spending it on therapy, on doctor bills. You will crack.

[At the office] you have to work harder than a man. You have to prove you're good, prove your abilities, [then] you gain respect. Some women are disrespectful to other women. [They say], "We did it, now you go ahead and do it."

We're committed to our kids, so we're spreading ourselves thin. We don't prioritize enough in terms of a couple, romantically. My husband and I, we make a conscious effort. We plan dates, we make time for each other; we do. He feels it's better for the kids. You have to find time together without the children to be able to just talk, to relate as man and wife. We schedule it, lunch or dinner or just two hours together. It took me time to learn this, to make dates. We bought a theater subscription. We try to make the magic come back.

The divorce rate, part of it is, I think, my generation is very me oriented, very selfish. If they're not getting what they want from their spouse, they're very ready to dissolve the union—as opposed to saying, "Maybe it's terrible now, but in six months things will get better. We're dealing with a real bad stretch." Like my sister, my brilliant sister. She divorced very quickly and after a couple of years of reflection, she said, "Maybe I was too impetuous."

I was born in the fifties and we've had some real bad stretches. When my son was born, I was nursing him and studying for exams. And I turned the bedroom into a library because I needed to pass this oral, come hell or high water, and we barely connected to each other. You go through it.

My husband is a nurturer to the kids, but not to me because he feels I am a partner, an equal partner. He made it very clear: "You're a big girl and you can take care of yourself. You're a capable woman, you're not going to play damsel in distress with me."

My passion is for my kids, to make them into mensches. You have to respect yourself first. It takes maturity. I wouldn't trade my life. I'm in a terrific place. I'm up at six, I don't go down till midnight. And I'm just grateful for what I have. I feel blessed.

While Nancy faced the ongoing effects of her child's catastrophic illness, and Cindy confronted relocation to Florida, her mother's death, and her husband's job loss, their coping strategies are very similar to Naomi's. They are looked upon by their spouses as equal partners, as capable and decisive adults. In addition, they are respected by their spouses as wage earners. These three women relinquish childrearing to their husbands when necessary, thereby giving up full control of the household, the traditional domain of Jewish female power. In restructuring the old power system, they acknowledge their husbands' abilities as nurturers and gain strength as a couple. While every marriage makes a unique footprint, these women balance work and love by demanding the best of themselves and their partners.

The conventional wisdom about stay-at-home moms used to be that they gave up employment to ensure the well-being of their children. They believed that working outside the home was detrimental. However, a University of Massachusetts study of more than six thousand youngsters found that a mother's working during the first three years of her child's life causes no harm.

However, for women in medicine, like Naomi, the road to compromise is the one most taken. Women cut their hours back to raise children, or put off having a family to avoid conflict. Many switch to practicing part time because the profession is so demanding. In the *workplace*, they accept less pay and prestige. The average female doctor earns $155,590 a year. The average male doctor earns $273,690. Bringing working mothers to the top of their professions is one challenge of the balancing act.

On the *home front*, Nancy, Cindy, and Naomi have tackled the issues decisively. Financial issues, health issues, job issues. To relieve themselves as primary nurturers to their children, they have enlisted their spouses.

This is a millennium paradigm we will see frequently: working moms and dads saying, "Money isn't everything." For example, a California survey asked 687 working men and women their number one career concern for the new millennium. The results showed that 23 percent wanted a competitive salary. But for 26 percent, "to balance work and family [was] their top career concern for the future."

Susan A. Glenn's book *Daughters of the Shtetl* tells us that immigrant daughters had limited ambitions, aspiring to marry out of the labor force and to be supported by a husband. They viewed work as a temporary interval between adolescence and marriage.

No more. Only a generation later, women have turned the working world around. As wage earners, they have forced bosses and companies to come to terms with family life as it is lived today.

A small company in New Jersey, for example, offers childcare and elder care consultations for between ten dollars and twenty-four dollars. One call to Work and Family Benefits does the legwork and provides a list of potential caregivers for employees to interview.

Today, mothers raising children work hard during the day, but they continue to protect their family time. And despite the juggling, they are thrilled to be productive, engaged, and challenged. Indeed, women in their thirties and forties have found men to be more willing partners in childrearing. Many dual-career families approach work and love as a team effort. And in the face of crises, they become masters of efficiency.

Of course, frustration and stress go with the territory. Working mothers become tightrope walkers, balancing children and jobs, husbands and bosses, personal issues and social issues that tax their energy. "Not easy, but doable" is what many say.

Renowned author Doris Kearns Goodwin tells us that when LBJ asked her how she managed so well to balance her time among work, love, and play, she answered: "there are going to be certain times in your life when you're not doing what you want to do especially when you have kids. There's the sense of wishing you had more time for the kids and yet not wanting your career to stagnate. It's most important to be easy on yourself . . . to remember that you do have a chance to catch up later in your life on what you might seem to have given up."

Nancy, Cindy, and Naomi are working mothers living that message. Balancing kids and jobs creates a frustrating challenge, deeply felt. But by choosing to have a family and a career, they are changing the world.

In the next chapter you'll hear *young single women* talk about what they expect and how they plan to balance families and work. Jewish husbands? How do you find them? Theirs is a different frustration. Are they hopelessly naive? Off the mark? Or right on target?

7

YOUNG
SINGLE WOMEN

MICHELLE

JODY

LILY

Do you know single Jewish women who are dying to get married but can't find a suitable candidate? I have two single nieces. Your mom's friend has a wonderful daughter. Everyone seems to knows a terrific woman—lawyers, doctors, programmers—out there doing the singles scene, and often you hear the same lament: "What men? There's aren't any available heterosexual males!"

Michael Segell, author of *Standup Guy: Masculinity That Works*, believes that women are still attracted to men who make more money than they do; [and] in fact, the more money women make, the *more* emphasis they place on the man's status. Consequently, "the higher women go, the more limited their choices become."

If this is true, *Jewish* women, traditionally well-educated and high achievers, face an even smaller pool to draw from. And if they are committed to limiting their husband search to a Jewish mate, that pool shrinks even more.

How do Jewish singles cope with the frustration?

What compromises do they make facing forty and desperately wanting a child?

Sara Davidson, author of the novel *Cowboy*, gives us an option/fantasy. A savvy Jewish divorcee, forty-nine, who is a successful Manhattan television writer, falls for a cowboy from Arizona who makes rawhide bridles, barely finished high school, and lives in a trailer. A classic case of "marrying down."

Is that the solution? Does desperation make strange bedfellows? And what are the chances of survival for such inappropriate liaisons? Davidson's novel is delightfully entertaining, but many would conclude that such couplings are unlikely to succeed in real life.

In this chapter you will meet three young, unmarried women who grapple with this dilemma. You will hear their expectations about their careers after they marry and have children. They speak about trade-offs that would be *un*acceptable and those that they would be *willing* to make.

Will they wind up with men making less money than they do, having less education than they have; and will they even select non-Jewish mates? It is a fear that strikes many Jewish hearts. If you're facing forty and you really want to marry, what compromises are appropriate?

First, you'll hear a sheltered Orthodox social worker, twenty-eight, describe the frenzy in New York to find a Jewish mate. Next, a Ph.D. candidate, twenty-nine, explains her logically laid out plans for managing a career and raising children. And finally, you'll meet a massage therapist, thirty-eight, working three part-time jobs, who is still on the look-out for Mr. Right.

Michelle

MICHELLE, 28, holds a B.S. in psychology, an A.A. in Judaic studies, and an M.S.W. from Wurzweiler School of Social Work, which is part of Yeshiva University. She lives alone in an Upper West Side apartment in Manhattan and commutes to her job as adult program director of a community center in New Jersey.

We meet in her office. She is a zaftig young woman in Calvin Klein jeans and leather boots, her makeup carefully applied and her blond curls cascading down her back.

She does a lot of hair touching and tossing, she giggles and sighs. She grew up in a modern Orthodox home; her parents were strictly kosher and forbade her to eat out.

"Pork? Ham? Shrimp? Never! The worst I ever did was dairy, like maybe pizza."

Michelle was a virgin until she slept with the man she married at twenty-two, her high school sweetheart. They were married four years and divorced; no children.

I FELT VERY *guilty sleeping with him without being married and I didn't want to live at home. You go to Stern [College], you look for a husband; it was the underlying message. You go to meet a nice Jewish boy. If you don't find a man in college, where are you going to find him?*

In New York [the scene] is thousands of young singles in their twenties and thirties desperately looking for a partner. I'm dating someone now and I mean, God, I'm going to be thirty soon. That sounds young. But to a man, they don't want thirty, they want twenty-five. So there's this fear, like the crop's drying up. And it's harder when you're out of college.

With the "X Generation" of twenty-somethings, it hasn't changed, not for religious Jewish singles. Once you're out of college, the selection is few and far between. Ninety-nine percent of my friends are married and having kids, there's no one to introduce you.

I know there's a lot of interfaith dating because I worked with college students before this job. Premarital sex was not an issue, and there was not the mad dash because there was not such a limited pool.

I look back now, seven years later, and I didn't know anything. A lot of religious girls like me are from sheltered families, and marriage is their only way to break out.

I blocked a lot about my marriage. Now that I'm dating someone seriously, a lot of stuff is coming back. How my husband told me he got married to have children young. I wanted to work and not have a child until I was twenty-seven and he felt deceived. He expected me to pop a baby out right away. He wanted me to take care of him like a mother. And he wasn't interested in sex; he was punishing me.

So by the end of our first year, I started to gain a lot of weight, I was eighty pounds heavier. I was like a big girl, a big girl. And he was gambling, obsessed with sports. If there was a game on, he wouldn't leave the house. He wouldn't give me a get, a Jewish divorce, and we went into therapy. But I wanted out and [finally] he didn't fight me, I got the get.

My mom's a physician, my dad too, and she always had live-in help. I expect to have children and go back to work. I still can't imagine staying home full time with a child. [But] I wouldn't want a nanny. I had a nanny growing up and that's what I don't want for my child. I don't want to repeat that. Never!

The man I'm seeing confirms what I feel; he doesn't believe in a nanny. He's Jewish, but not religious. He would send his children to an Orthodox yeshiva, but he's not shomar Shabbos. He's nine years older, a professor, and a klezmer musician. He's got a CD out and does gigs on Friday nights and Saturday. It bothers me. He doesn't see himself as becoming more religious and I can't get in a car on shabbos. Never. I walk to OZ. That's Oheb Zedek on Ninety-fifth Street, the Jewish meat market.

On Friday night after services, everyone blocks up the street, seven hundred Jewish men and women socializing, maybe twenty-three to thirty-five, everyone looking their best, out to be seen, to meet someone, to get invited to a meal.

It's not a matchmaking service, but everyone's looking—you might meet Mr. or Ms. Right. I know marriages that came out of it, oh yes. I'm not putting it down, but people have to look beyond the exterior. There's a lot of women that you expect are virgins that are not virgins. And the men exclude divorced women, they want the image of this young pretty thing on their arm—the exterior, not the interior. It makes me sad, a sad scene to see. They should be looking for someone with the same values.

I look at my friends who got married and have children and they're so settled. It's what I want at forty, not twenty-eight, so we don't have anything to say anymore. And my single friends are still looking for a man. Not me. We talk on the phone, we share experiences, we keep in touch. For Jewish women, it's hard. But there's a lot of programming in the city for singles.

There's Hineni. It means "here I am." On Tuesday nights, fifteen hundred to two thousand young singles ages twenty-one to thirty-five get together. It's a social hour and they have a building on West End Avenue and Seventieth. The Hineni Building. Rebbetzin Esther Jungreis talks about the weekly Torah portion; she's a motivational speaker, like a guru. And she writes a weekly column in the Jewish press about dating and marriage. There's an optional five-dollar donation. There's soda and chips, a social hour to mingle, and they hang out in the hall and check everyone out. A big single scene.

Thursday is an older crowd, thirty-five to fifty. People who come are not necessarily religious; it's more those who want to return to the faith and become more religious. Bal tshuva, [it means] "a return to spirituality." It's not the meat market of OZ with the guise of praying. OZ, you go there to be seen. Hineni is more honest, and the lectures are very dynamic and something to think about. And they have events like retreats and parties and trips to Israel. There's a free matchmaking service, someone sitting there to do a bio of you and what you're looking for. It's more respectable and successful with singles who aren't religious.

My own expectations, like for when I'm married and have children—I can't see myself staying home, no. But I'd have to see the quality of care *that's available. The man I'm seeing wants children and I do see him as a partner in childrearing.*

I would never want to give up working full time. God forbid something happens. It's the sense of inner security. I'm not in a high-powered job, he makes more than me. I work for the satisfaction more than the money.

My [former] roommate wants to stay home and raise a child. Two of my friends are making more money than their husbands and they have to work to keep up their lifestyle. I think women want options. But realistically, they can't drop out of the workforce and go back, no. You lose too much. Out of work a year, a year and a half—past that it's a hurdle to get back and you're not respected as a serious contender. It hurts you.

I think women can have it all. It means to feel complete in all aspects of your life, as a worker and as a wife. Having it all can mean being a housewife. To me it's having healthy children influenced by me and my husband, who is a partner. And having a satisfying job where the employer has childcare.

With religious single women, it's harder. I don't see that changing. Yes, religion makes it harder and more complicated. But it's not undoable.

Michelle gives us a vivid picture of life as a single Jewish woman in New York, a very special category. However, we hear the same concerns echoed by women in suburbia and in other cities. Men complain that Jewish women expect to be taken care of; and women complain that Jewish men are marrying women who are willing to take care of them. An article in *Metrowest* (N.J.) *Jewish News* again raises the question: have Jewish women "priced themselves out of reach of the nice Jewish boys they claim they really want?"

Several months after this interview took place, I saw Michelle. Her blond curls were chopped off and her smile was radiant. She showed me her engagement ring. "Yes, the professor!" She is leaving her apartment in New York and buying a home in New Jersey close to her job.

Jody

JODY, 29, is a Ph.D. candidate from Indianapolis. She is tall and sleek, with a lovely smile, and she is as dark and exotic as Michelle is blond and girlish. And she is not Orthodox.

"Our Reform temple merged with the Conservative and we became Reformative," she laughs. "But I'm more secular and agnostic. I don't have faith in some mystical power."

Jody describes herself as a part-time research assistant and a full-time student. At Tufts University, where she earned her B.S. in clinical psychology, she turned sour on organized religion.

"But I have this very strong sense of my heritage and I want to date Jewish. In Indianapolis, surrounded by non-Jews, I feel even more Jewish."

With an M.S. in clinical rehabilitation psychology, Jody is now at Indiana University Purdue University Indianapolis (IUPUI) in a demanding Ph.D. program that focuses on chronic disorders.

"I have two more practica to finish up and I'm starting work on my dissertation proposal. I'm quite nervous."

Jody is also working a twenty-hour week for her research advisor/mentor. The job becomes full time over the summer—a seventy- to eighty-hour week, counting the academic and clinical work.

I'M THRILLED WITH *my mentor, I love what I do. We just finished a project for the Illinois Department of Mental Health on psychosocial rehabilitation. Which means helping people with severe mental illness gain employment. It involved site visits, being on the road, interviewing staff at health centers, then doing the data analysis, and writing up the report.*

I'm a perfectionist and there's something so pleasant about data and numbers—the process of turning chaos into something neat and orderly.

I get a lot of pleasure out of taking something complicated and making it simple. And I know everything I do has a higher purpose — helping people with severe disorders to function better. It's messy and dirty and hard and frustrating. And that adds to the challenge!

The guy I recently broke up with was a doctor, and finding time to be together was difficult. It compromised my sleep and my schedule. He was rigid and I had to bend, so the relationship ended. [But] I definitely *want to be married.*

I find being single to be hard. I don't feel the biological clock ticking, no, but I'd like a partner. I see myself having children, but not for a long time. I'm so committed to work, to the Ph.D., that the balancing would be too tough.

However, I'm changing. My mindset about life and work is changing. For example, I'm planning a vacation in March, dropping everything in the middle of the semester and spending money I don't have. And I don't care. It may be the thirtieth birthday coming up. I work too hard.

Traditionally, this is a male field, [but] we're actively recruiting women and not finding anyone. My degree is a very flexible degree; it allows people to do private practice or academic or a nine-to-five job. Women aren't doing the tenure track because there are other opportunities that are more family friendly. Getting tenure and having babies is too hard. Unless the husband stays home and is Mr. Mom. [But] there's still the guilt. My male mentor has a wife with a Ph.D. and she stays home. I'd be resentful. Without a doubt!

Expectations? I try very hard to date Jewish, I make the effort. I'd want my husband to support my work. I feel now is the time to publish and go for grants. Mostly it feels good to be work oriented. But I also feel the loneliness of being single. Yet moving in with someone and losing my space, well, if the relationship ended . . . ?

I don't understand my single friends who can't wait to have babies. I think I want children, but I don't want them now. I have a picture of what would be ideal: to marry someone who has a flexible job or worked at home or part-time, so he could take an active role in child-raising. I tend to be pretty picky. I look for a life partner when I date, not someone to hang out with. Maybe I need to change that. Most of my friends in Indianapolis are partnered and having babies. I'd like a partner.

There's a singles organization [here], part of the JCC, and [you see] the same people, the same faces. The events, are not terribly successful. Four synagogues have events, but I don't attend. The JCC started a matchmaker organization of volunteers trained by a psychologist, but they told me, "Sorry, there's nobody here who's appropriate." I just don't know.

Do Jewish women expect too much? I wonder about that. If we're educated and goal oriented, we expect to marry someone as successful. Jewish women are not going to marry down. No, they're going to marry up. And if you're already up, it's hard to find that much more up. Unlikely I'm going to marry a plumber or a laborer. I'm not looking for money, but someone intellectually stimulating.

On the other side, you're Jewish: you have to be a good mother and family oriented. God only knows how we can do that balancing act. The whole thing is scary, an impossible mountain to climb. What I fear is finding an unacceptable partner, being in a situation where I have to make a hard decision about family or career. Finding someone is hard, but I don't think Jewish women are too picky. No! But being Jewish makes it harder.

I wonder how can I possibly think that someone is going to walk into my life and be single, be educated, be flexible, and be family oriented, someone who supports my work. How in God's name does someone exist like that? And then I see my friends meet them. So I think they have to be out there somewhere.

With the rise of technology and the Internet—well, I just got an e-mail from somebody in Toronto [from] an ad I put out when I broke up. And it astounds me! People [from] all over who feel they can't meet anyone. There's a huge Jewish population in Toronto, huge! And he says he can't meet anyone in Toronto. It doesn't make sense.

If we're all out there, why aren't we meeting?

Remember the *Newsweek* article that struck fear into the hearts of unmmarried women? It said you had a better chance of being kidnapped by terrorists than finding a husband if you're over thirty-five. With marriage age rising and with Jews having high rates of graduate school attendance, Jewish anxiety seems to be rising. To stem the fears, community centers and synagogues are presenting a variety of events, programs, and matchmaker services. Which, some claim, foster even *more* anxiety.

Many psychologists believe that most Jewish women who want to marry, will. And if they've used their single years to grow intellectually and emotionally, empowering themselves, they will bring richness to the marriage at whatever age that occurs.

However, while they're single many women are living *real* lives— not living "in the meantime" lives, hoping Mr. Right will rescue them. They have good friends, they travel, they have work they enjoy. Like Jody, they aren't standing around waiting for the phone to ring.

And some are actually saying, "Single? I prefer it, that's my choice."

A highly successful, single, freelance writer phoned me from her assignment in London. She told me this: "Work is better than sex for some women. I've given up on marriage, but not on love. I'd rather do my work than work at making some man happy."

When I called back, hoping to set up an interview, she had already flown off to Morocco to do a piece in Marrakech.

Lily

LILY, 38, is a massage therapist working three part-time jobs. She is a tall blond with trusting light gray eyes and a soothing calmness. She has a soft, caressing voice. She's wearing a white medical jacket when we meet at the JCC Health Club where she was hired seven years ago, her first therapy job.

Lily lives with her parents, who raised her in a Conservative Jewish home. After her bat mitzvah, she stopped Hebrew school.

A graduate of the Morris Institute of Natural Therapeutics, she studied for three months to be certified in Swedish massage.

"My high school years were tough and I got disillusioned. I didn't want to waste my parents' money on college."

After high school, she worked as a hostess in a restaurant, office manager in a furniture store, and then office manager for a physical therapist, who advised her to study physical therapy.

"[But] I don't test well and I didn't have confidence in the sciences, so [I went] for massage."

Today Lily boasts a list of loyal clients in three locations: at the JCC Health Club, where she sees regular clients by appointment; at the full-service beauty salon located close to the Health Club; and at the prestigious Hilton Spa, where she works on Sundays.

I HAVE A nice following. And I like the variety. I used to visit clients in their home, do a massage party for five or six women. But it was getting hard on my back, shlepping the table and lotions and towels. Gotta have some free time.

The satisfaction of my work is helping people feel better. Massage is so good for you in so many ways. Immediately, I see the results. I can feel it in their muscle tone and see it on their faces. I just love it.

A lot of therapists open their own places and that's nice, the potential to make lots of money. But I'd have to give up my clients and [have] the headache of hiring people; they don't show up. I know I can depend on myself. It doesn't appeal to me.

Dating? I've never had any luck with Jewish men and my parents are open minded enough that if I married outside the religion, at least he would be a good person. In my family we have examples of mixed marriages that worked.

For me, the Jewish men were JAPpy—Jewish American Princes. I'm not so materialistic, I'm down-to-earth. And a lot of the men are whiny. I *like men who are handy with their hands. [With] Jewish men, the wife becomes the mother figure, always cooking and cleaning and having food on the table. It's a second-class position. I have a lot of nurturing in me, but I'm not going to be their mother.*

I want to continue working. There's nothing wrong with the traditional housewife role, but it's not for me. I don't want someone dominant over me. My expectation is definitely to continue working. To give it up would hurt me.

Children? I'm thirty-eight now, and even though women are having babies later, thank God, and healthy, that's still a possibility for me. But I'm not going to marry someone just to have a baby. I can't afford to bring a baby into this world alone and I don't think it's fair. It's better to have two parents.

If I don't, I don't. I would love it, I haven't totally ruled it out. But if I don't, I have two beautiful nieces, and there's always adoption. It's a regret I haven't had children, but it's not a big pressure. I think about it from time to time. If I don't have children, it will be a little sadness. I would fill it with other things. And one day I might be in a different position to take on a child and adopt. Or [find] a man with children from another marriage—well, that's another whole bag. I won't know until I'm in that position.

To meet guys, I tend to rely on friends and relatives; even clients have fixed me up. There's something cold about doing it on the Internet or the newspaper. You have to be careful. I ended up going out once with a pervert. You have to protect yourself, meet in a public place. I go to a diner or for coffee; I try to keep it short and sweet. A picnic, no, that's too intimate on a first date. I can size up a guy, and my friends yell at me I discount them too quick. But it's a feeling, a perception, like, the guy who turned out to be a pervert. He turned it into phone sex and I'm like, "Excuse me!"

My mother's friends have given my number out, but it didn't work. The chemistry wasn't there.

When you have children, it's important to be with them, if you can afford it. I know good situations, and I know bad situations where the child is shuffled back between grandmothers and nannies. My mom was home for me and I liked it. But it's a totally different world and most families need two incomes. It's good for the mom to have a little part-time job on the side to get her out and feel she's still a person. If I had a child, I'd give up working for a while, definitely until school age.

I've done the Jewish single dances—they're losers. I met one guy, laid off, who was doing temp work; he wanted to be a stand-up comedian. And he was growing on me. [But] he didn't have a car, he lived in New York, and when I came from work to see him in a show, he didn't even offer me something to eat. So I crossed him off my list. Cheap. And this was a nice Jewish boy.

I also had a two- to three-year relationship with a Jewish guy who was divorced, very hurt. I had to try to prove I wouldn't hurt him. He was floundering in his career. He hooked up with the wrong people and ended up with a drug problem.

Yes, the Jewish community is reaching out, but I don't know. Single dances, people are desperate to hook up and hop in the sack. I went to a dinner thing too. Yucky. You see the same people again and again. First dates feel like an interview, you get the third degree.

For fun, I go out with my girlfriends, theater, a weekend to Philly, sightseeing, a cruise. I think when I finally meet someone it will be at a wedding or a party, you know, "across a crowded room." I have friendships among my massage colleagues. [But] only 5, 10 percent are Jewish. It doesn't bother me.

I see clients at all levels, women with very good jobs, [who] threaten a man with their independence. And some men don't know what they want; they're immature. I'd want a man with a steady job. I expect him to be the provider, but I'd help along.

Intelligence is a turn-on to me. Good looks help, but the more you like someone, they become attractive. If a guy turned me on and didn't want children . . . well, I'm getting older. The baby thing is not a priority for me anymore. My plans have changed.

*Even if I married out of the religion, I would never consider convert-
ing. We'd practice both religions. The children? That would be a tough
one.*

*I'm a flexible person. He doesn't have to be Jewish. We don't have to
have children.*

Lily's expectations are clearly quite different from Jody's and Michelle's.
At thirty-eight, she has made accommodations about balancing work
and love.

She wants a man with a steady job, a provider; but she would help
make ends meet. Consider how wide the chasm is between her and
Jody, so fervently dedicated to her research work, and Michelle, who
can't imagine staying home full time. Both Jody and Michelle require
a partner in parenting and a man supportive of their work.

What factors separate these three? Is it merely age? Does a decade of
dashed dreams restructure the expectations of single women? Does
facing forty carve out compromises? "He doesn't have to be Jewish. We
don't have to have children," Lily concludes.

Will Jody and Michelle arrive at that point?

Lily's compromises are not unusual. I've heard them discussed
among mothers of unmarried daughters (and sons) who shrug and say,
"I only want to see her happy." Lily calls it "flexibility."

On the other hand, age is not the only factor. Lily has a high school education. In Jewish families, daughters who have *not* gone to college are a
tiny minority. The level of a woman's education may limit her choices.

In fact, I was frustrated trying to set up interviews with Jewish
women in blue-collar jobs: waitresses, check-out clerks, factory workers. I walked through K-mart looking for a Star of David. I checked
supermarket employees. And I finally called a synagogue in an eco-
nomically depressed town and asked them for help. Result? The Sisterhood president could not locate a single congregant who had not been
to college, and several held graduate degrees.

Of course, the opposite holds true as well. Jody tells us highly educated women won't "marry down," and "if you're already up, it's hard to find that much more up." Michelle tells us Orthodox women face a shrinking pool of available men. This is the dilemma of Jewish singles. To accommodate? To remain purists? To seek family-friendly employers in the workforce? To expect shared parenting from husbands? To sacrifice ambition to raise children? To go part time for family reasons? Or to revise their expectations about balancing work and family life?

Do you remember Bette Midler in the film *Beaches*? As C. C. Bloom, she goes to her mother for comfort because her marriage is falling apart. And her mother (Lainie Kazan) angrily lets her have it. "You always wanted too much attention!" That's her analysis.

Do Jewish women demand too much attention? Too many material goods? Too much achievement? Too much emotional support from their partners? Too many benefits in the workplace? Do Jewish women, reared with high expectations for themselves and others, simply expect too much?

Some Jewish women will be single because they couldn't find a suitable partner. Others will choose the single life rather than the *huppa*. Seeking satisfaction through work and friends, single women are traveling, whale watching, mountain climbing, and making their own feminist seders.

Since 1970, the number of single women living alone has doubled. And first-time brides over forty don't even raise an eyebrow. To some extent the media has supported this trend. *The Mary Tyler Moore Show* of the 1970s established Mary Richards's workplace, a TV station, as a source of family warmth and friendship. "Single women working in the office" emerged as a popular theme for TV shows—a trend subsequently reconfirmed by the long life of TV series, *Murphy Brown*.

And for those who want to *end* a marriage, the tide is also turning. Once, Orthodox women in unsatisfactory marriages had no recourse. Like Michelle, if their husband refused to grant a *get*, they stayed married. Not any more. Several Orthodox rabbis have declared that there is ample precedent for granting annulments in Jewish law—that such annulments conform to halacha, the body of law that governs Jewish life. For Orthodox wives, obtaining a divorce is becoming less difficult. But divorce brings a new set of pressures to working women.

In the next chapter you will meet four *single moms raising children alone*. They, too, had plans. But divorce forced them to take another route. A sharp contrast to their hopes and dreams.

8

SINGLE MOMS RAISING CHILDREN ALONE

MARIAN

BARBARA

KAREN

WENDY

For separated and divorced working mothers, the struggle to balance work and love becomes even harder. Having to raise their children alone invites depression and anger. Having to hold down a job to pay the rent invites fatigue and stress.

How do they do it?

How do single moms manage when the challenges intensify? How do their children fare? Battling regrets and recriminations, how do single moms survive the pain and manage financially and emotionally?

In this chapter, *four* single moms tell us how they had to swerve and spin to keep their balance. How their lifestyles changed, how they tapped into new strengths, and how they emerged out of that dark tunnel as different people.

Marian

Marian, 57, is a hearty, graying midwesterner married to her second husband for nine years. She has honest brown eyes and wears a no-nonsense wash-and-wear haircut and little makeup.

Her journey from neat-freak housewife to confident entrepreneur includes two divorces from her first husband, which thrust her into being a single mom raising two daughters, and forced her from her upscale suburban lifestyle into a tiny rented apartment in Cincinnati.

"I loved being a mom and none of my friends worked outside the home—it wasn't the thing in the sixties," she says, rubbing the arms of her fisherman's sweater.

Today Marian is a new grandmother. But she remembers the struggle.

I WAS DOING *interior design after college, which I loved. I graduated with a B.A. in English from the University of Cincinnati and got married at twenty-three. We had two girls and I quit to raise them. My husband didn't want me to work.*

So what did I do? I cleaned my house every day. I was absolutely anal-compulsive, a neat freak to the point where one day he cut my vacuum-cleaner cord. Came up with a scissors, pulled out the plug and cut it. I kid you not. We were already having marital problems, a lot of friction. I had to drag him on the Jewish holidays, he was even less observant than me.

In the sixties, we were housewives and a lot of us wound up in bad marriages, getting divorced in our late thirties. [After] we got divorced the second time—the remarriage lasted a year—I had to go to work, I needed the money. The kids were in school all day, but I made sure my working didn't impact on them. I took them to school and I picked them up at three. I [took] part time, ten to two, at the Jewish Community Relations Council. Work felt good. I kept thinking, Thank God I have this job. I worked four hours, then turned into "mom." It was a good kind of exhaustion.

Greater Cincinnati is about half a million and the Jewish community is not very large. I was working with newspapers and I ran a speakers bureau and I set up functions when dignitaries came from Israel. Public relations. The attention and adulation I got was spectacular.

After three years I went to full time because I didn't feel I had to be home at three. I was a single mom raising two kids, one in junior high and one in high school. When I left, my confidence level had grown so much I felt like I could sell ice cubes to Eskimos.

[For one year] I took a job with a large brokerage company as director of public relations. [But I hated] commuting thirteen miles to downtown Cincinnati and back again, so I left [for] a job with a bank which is now PNC. They put me in the loan department and I worked there five years. I had no idea; I was totally out of my element, and it was a source of nightmares. I was making loans to wealthy people, some in their sixties, waiting for their elderly parents to die and leave them money. The stress level was high and child support was running out and I had to support myself. So I stayed.

By then I had given up my 3,000-square-foot home with four bedrooms and three bathrooms, in a beautiful neighborhood, for a 750-square-foot apartment in the city. And you know what? By this time I loved the fact that I was taking care of myself. I felt totally empowered.

I decorated it and I made it as cute as you can imagine. A tiny rented apartment overlooking the Ohio River. A lovely view. It felt like my first nest. I was starting fresh.

I was forty-five and I definitely wanted to get married again. I was dating ten years, so many jerks I had finally given up. I always thought I needed a man to complete myself, that was the scenario we were taught. I wanted a man, but I didn't need one, and I had a tremendous circle of women friends.

Then, at forty-eight, I met my second husband. I found my soul mate, a man who accepted me totally for who I am. I was still working at the bank and hating it. He's a lawyer, also divorced, and he loved his work. He showed me that I could quit and get a job I really loved. Which was to do interior design.

So a friend and I decided to market ourselves as a team. We joined a four-woman design firm and I stayed five years. Frankly, at this point I didn't need the money, my husband was supporting us. I was working for validation. So I left that firm to go out on my own and I took my clients with me.

I opened my own business out of my home. I am the sole owner. And if someone had told me twenty years ago I'd make five dollars on my own, I'd have called them crazy. My husband loved seeing me come home smiling. We took a larger apartment, my children and his were grown, and I set up my business at home.

I truly admire the feminists who fought to get where we are today. But I do not feel that women can have it all—well, there are exceptions. Either have your children and postpone your career, or have your career and postpone your children. I think women who try to have it all compromise their children. My daughter still remembers in high school how when I was off from work I could come and get her. She liked that, she liked my being home after school, that I was in the house.

Women who say they're having it all—I'm going to go out on a limb— I think they're fooling themselves. Their children miss something, and they'll look back on it and say differently. If they have to work, okay, if they have to put food on the table.

When I was working full time there were moments of guilt, but I had to do it. My daughters went through some very hard times with me; it was a stressful divorce. Jewish women feel mothers should be with their children and this delivers more conflict and guilt.

Right now Jewishness impacts very little on us. Except as nostalgic memories. We don't observe Jewish holidays and we have become disenchanted with Israel. And because the Federation is so strongly pro-Israel, we give less to Jewish causes and more to other causes like Planned Parenthood, AIDS, the Negro College Fund and cancer.

My oldest daughter is married to a Jewish boy. They light candles on Friday night. It absolutely surprises me!

Like Marian, working moms often say, "I had to go to work, we needed the money." It is a fact that following divorce, a woman's quality of life decreases dramatically while the man's is more likely to stay the same or improve. Many divorced moms, finding themselves financially strapped, are forced to take part-time, low-paying jobs. Or, like Marian, they take jobs they don't like.

Of course, Marian was fortunate. Despite some hard knocks, she emerged as a strong, independent woman and a successful entrepreneur. Consider Marian's move from an elegant suburban home to a tiny city apartment. Bitter pills for some; for others, opportunity. "I loved the fact that I was taking care of myself. . . . I felt totally empowered."

Barbara

BARBARA, 53, was plunged into being a single mom when her husband fell out of love with her. Like Marian, she used this period in her life to transform herself.

Mother of two daughters, 28 and 25, she holds a master's in education and is now program administrator in early childhood at a New Jersey JCC. She has not remarried. Her husband has.

Black is her uniform. Her small, wiry frame is sheathed in black slacks, black turtleneck, and black loafers. Her hair is a shiny black helmet under which a pair of intelligent dark eyes peer out.

Though she appears upbeat, there's a quiet sadness in her voice when she explains how her "tight" family unraveled when she won the coveted job she set out to get and her husband was asked to leave his highly successful CPA firm.

"I felt really great. He felt pretty low. That's when the change came."

We are seated in her cluttered office with the sounds of three- and four-year-olds lining up for dismissal, singing "Put your finger on the wall, on the wall."

I WAS BROUGHT up in upper Manhattan in a Conservative home, but we kept kosher and we went to temple. My brother was bar mitzvahed, not me.

Both of my daughters were bat mitzvahed. And as adults they have carried forward what they learned. They work very hard to be with me on Jewish holidays, as opposed to their father, because he remarried someone not Jewish. But they go to him the second night of Rosh Hashanah. I feel I am a religious person. I remember the rabbi teaching us "Religion is in your heart."

When I was sixteen I went to Israel to meet my relatives. Most of them fled from Germany. I met my only grandparent there. I spent the whole summer, I went from cousin to cousin. My second trip was in a professional capacity; wonderful, but different.

I graduated from Long Island University and I got married the same year. I was twenty-one. We knew each other since we were sixteen and we were very much in love. I still think he's a wonderful guy and a wonderful father. But if I hadn't divorced him, I wouldn't be the person I am today. Because when you're alone, you learn much more about yourself and you take charge.

He was the stronger one and I was adaptable to his needs. His philosophy in life was to have good things. We had Mercedes, Jaguars, an apartment in Aspen, a house in St. Marten—those things were important to him. To me, experiences were more important, [not] material things. It was one of the problems in our marriage.

My husband built up this accountant firm from four people to hundreds. What happened, there was a schism in the firm and he was asked to leave. And his ego, which was extremely large at that point, was deflated. I was angry because I felt if we hadn't bought all those things and we had saved money, which is my philosophy, we wouldn't be in that [financial] situation. There was a lot of anger.

I said, "We have to sell this house, we can't afford to live here."

That was a terrible thing to him because the house was wrapped up in his ego. Also, he had loaned money to the firm and taken out another mortgage, so we had an astronomical mortgage and second mortgage and we couldn't get the money back.

I was teaching part time. Financially, there was no reason to work full time. But now I took a second job to at least have the security of medical insurance for my family. I ran a kindergarten program that was extremely rewarding. I created the program and it fulfilled so much for me. I took the children to museums, I did art tours. But my children came first. It was the reason I chose the job: flexibility. I got up every morning and I wanted to go to work, a great feeling. But it was clear that my husband was the breadwinner.

We were married twenty-seven years. When I started to work more, he had a hard time with that. I became a salesperson on the weekends and he felt that was beneath me. I said I wanted it for financial reasons, but actually I was happier being by myself. I used the work as an excuse. I said, "You go skiing, have a good time." I was avoiding a confrontation and it was a way of not focusing on our problems. My memory was our sex life was good. His memory was it was not.

Recently, I went back to college for my learning disability certification, with the intention of starting a private practice. I think about it every day. It's my dream. But somehow, I'm avoiding the starting step.

Feminism has been very important for me; I read feminist articles and books. My father was a very arrogant man and my mother felt subservient to him. That is just not acceptable to me. My mother is ninety-three and greatly disappointed that I got divorced. She's concerned about me. She's helped me financially. I was in control of a trust fund she provided; that's how our children went to college. My mother would like to know I'm happy before she dies.

So why did I take on another job nine years ago, knowing it would not please my husband? I didn't go after this job. He was traveling a lot for clients and a friend asked me to come to her store. We had sold the house and moved into a rented condo. I did it one weekend and it was kinda fun, the clothes were fabulous. It just happened.

But I did go after this JCC job, the one I hold now! It was the most aggressive thing I ever did in my whole life. I really wanted it, I was so excited. It was a turning point for me. I felt really great and he felt really low. That's when the change came. He said he fell out of love with me.

That's simplistic. I wasn't feeding his ego. He's a very good-looking guy, charming, tall, and [he met] this woman who had very little education and was left with a baby. Well, here comes this very caring guy. I can understand it.

My daughters and I have a very close relationship. My older daughter lives with her boyfriend, but she's not ready to get married. I feel that has something to do with our divorce. Our divorce was a shock for our children. We were a tight family.

It's interesting. My daughter only sees me as the person I am today—how I live alone and I love having my own space. But I wasn't like this when I was her age. I'm only like this now. She doesn't remember who I was. The message she got is from who I am today. She's a headhunter and very serious about her work, and she sees me as a role model. I'm in charge of forty teachers in staff and 350 children in the basic nursery school, plus parenting classes and much more.

I talk to these younger women, and it's wonderful to see them juggling being a parent and working. Some of them have fabulous occupations—they're television directors, doctors, and lawyers. And very caring [parents]. It's part of our Jewish value system. It's our history.

The most stressful area of balancing [work and love] is the physical part, having enough energy and time to be positive with your children. I see that. Some mothers can stay home and make a good choice, but they've got to find that thing that will give them the self-esteem.

I think it's important for women to have something that's their own, something they're doing for themselves. Being a parent is the most important job. But for your own self-esteem, you must have that intellectual stimulation in your life.

All my friends are working women. I have strong female relationships and I don't know how I'd survive without that. I have wonderful people in my life. Also I exercise to relieve stress, I work out every morning. I'm a happy person because I have that in my life.

I just ended a relationship with a man who wanted me more of the time than I was able to give. Wrong person? Or am I not able to trust a man again? I don't know. Too many females have been taught to be passive.

My largest challenge as a working woman is to make sure I'll be secure in my old age. What's going to happen when I'm older if I don't meet someone to share my life with?

Barbara got her present job because "it was the most aggressive thing I ever did." She went after it. "Too many females have been taught to be passive," she comments. Something she learned *after* her divorce.

Some might argue that her jobs cost her her marriage. Others will point to her husband's lifestyle of Jaguars and apartments in Aspen. Still others will argue that their values were at odds. Or that his job loss required a boost to his ego: a new wife. Rarely is there one factor in a divorce, although single moms, looking back, may focus on one.

However, in almost all cases, there is guilt.

Are the children harmed? Do adult children of divorced parents hesitate about marriage because they've witnessed their parents' failure? Barbara feels that her daughter's reluctance to get married, "has something to do with our divorce."

Finally, we must pay heed to what many single moms in the workplace say about their female friends. While burdened with guilt, financial pressures, and workplace stress, single moms raising children alone need comfort and to whom do they go? Their women friends, of course. Who else understands them so well? "I have strong female relationships and I don't know how I'd survive without that."

And yet, despite the strengths she's acquired as a single working woman, Barbara still worries about her future. "What's going to happen when I'm older if I don't meet someone to share my life with?"

Karen

KAREN, 48, is a fundraiser for a Jewish agency and a single mom raising two teenage sons. Separated two years, she came from a Conservative home, but is now Reform.

"Identity and spirituality came to me in my thirties," she says; then adds, "I went to Israel two years ago and I'm absolutely committed to getting [my children] there."

At five foot two, she weighs about one hundred pounds, has long, straight brown hair, and could easily be taken to be in her mid-thirties. An elfin, twinkly woman, soft voiced but certainly not diffident, she knows who she is. She wears a long black skirt and a tan turtleneck and her hazel green eyes are thoughtful. She offers no quick answers.

With a master's in museum practices, Karen's goal was to be director of a medium-sized art museum. Her husband worked as director of production for a book publisher. They lived in Indianapolis.

I GREW UP in Detroit and worked full time for various museums until my first son was born. I'm from the Midwest so I was raised with different values. I was on a career track. But once I had my son, I changed. I went back three times trying to work out a balance, and I found it was too demanding. My husband didn't understand.

I began Zen shortly after we separated because I wanted a way to empty my mind and relax, to bring spirituality into my life. I was very involved with my temple, on the board and very active. But when we separated, it was like all of a sudden I didn't exist because we weren't a couple. There was no support, they didn't call, nobody said, "What happened?" So I left. And I began Zen Vipassana, which is insight meditation. It's helped me enormously.

From the start, neither one of us were good with money. My husband had a business that went bankrupt and for a while we did very badly. We both worked but we didn't manage our money, we didn't plan, we didn't save. We were going into a lot of debt.

Six months after my first son was born I went back to work full time at the museum. I'd run home at lunchtime to breast-feed him, and I'd pump in my office. One of the board members took me aside and said. "Look. We expected you to come back full of energy." I worked six months more and I saw my son bond with the nanny more than with me. So I quit.

My husband was disappointed. His mother always worked and had a nanny. He didn't understand the importance of family to me. My husband was well intentioned, he helped me out with diaper changes. But he encouraged me to work.

There was not enough communication. If I wasn't interested in sex, he'd just say "Okay." That was part of our problem. There was loneliness and we were both constantly stressed. We didn't discuss, we just drifted further apart. I'd try to reach out to him, but that was not his style. We even went to counseling for six months; it wasn't useful. He wanted to mend the marriage. He still does.

And he's very fair with financial support. But I probably shouldn't have married him, we weren't right from the beginning. I was twenty-eight. The marriage lasted eighteen years.

When we met, I was so ambitious. But once I had children, my values changed. His didn't. And I didn't discuss [it], not really, because I knew he didn't understand.

When I finally quit the museum, I wanted something flexible. It wasn't a decision to go into public relations, I just wanted to be able to leave and pick up my kids. I struggled with it for years and I decided my first priority was my children, the job would have to fit around them.

The defining moment for me was when I had an abortion because my husband didn't want a third child. I did it for him. That was a low for me. Our younger son was three and I was angry for so many years. That was just another piece of it.

Now that we're apart, he's maturing. Funny to say, he's almost fifty and I see some changes. We continue to talk about the marriage, but I'm in no rush because I'm not afraid of being alone. It's a little scary, but I'm moving up professionally, I'm feeling pretty strong.

Sure, my boys are impacted, I couldn't say they're not. But I make sure I'm visible at home; there's a lot of stability in our life. We talk a lot, I put nice dinners on the table, I want to be caring and responsible. I think I have well-adjusted children, they're high achievers. They express their sadness about their dad and I tell them, "I understand, but I can't fix it."

I remember watching stay-at-home moms on television; and I think, balancing work and family—it's different for everyone. There are going to be women who are better moms because they're working and they feel fulfilled. And there are going to be women who want to stay home, and you have to go with your gut.

I'm in line for a promotion and I think the time is right for me. My kids are on their way and I work where there is flexibility, so if my kids need me, that's understood. I'll be getting paid more and my plan is that in five or six years, when the boys are in college, I'll go to New York and really do well.

But right now this is perfect. I waited. I was patient.

I think we've been sold a bill of goods. We think we can have it all. But at some point it just hits you in the face.

Our Jewish values tell us we have certain obligations to the home and the family. But the reality is you are expected to have a certain house and success and to live up to that pressure. I tried really hard. Maybe it helps because I'm from the Midwest, born in Windsor, Michigan, so I came out with different values.

Today, if you do volunteer work, you're expected to have the material stuff and the meetings at your house. You pull up into this long circular driveway, and you have this little bungalow. Living in an upscale Jewish community, there's a lot of pressure to look good. But you can't always afford it. So women try to make more money. It's sad, but we're too materialistic; it's the pressure to [have] all the trappings. I'd go to dinners and I couldn't participate in the conversations, it was all about vacations. Well, we couldn't afford to travel.

I became a leader anyhow, but I was embarrassed. We had this little home that was not nicely kept up and it was a stark difference to [their] enormous houses. I struggle with this. To find a good compromise [and] be a caring and competent parent.

There's not enough opportunities for women. We have to work harder than a man to achieve our goals. And working women who don't have children to raise are not very understanding.

Yesterday I had a meeting with my director, a man. He got up and said, "I have to leave now to take my daughter to ballet and my son to soccer." And I made a mental note of that. It showed me I can do that. Men are learning the pressures because we are interchanging roles.

My mom felt totally unempowered because she never worked. She told me, "There were times I wanted to leave your dad but I just couldn't."

I know I struggled to perceive my own empowerment. I kept thinking, I can't do this. Then I remind myself that I am doing this, that I'm coping and I'm competent.

[With Zen], I've tapped something in me I didn't know was available: the positive energy of meditation. It comes back to that. I'm learning life truths and it's helping me get through the garbage. I can see more clearly.

Raising two teenagers alone and working, the hardest part is I wish I could do more for them. Everyone seems to be doing more. I wish I could afford to send them to better camps, a college fund, what money buys. They deserve it. They get enough love and attention. We're okay.

And I get what I need for myself. I start every day meditating and [then] working out. I'm committed to that. A half hour every morning. If you can become "in the moment" and get the essence of reality, you realize that all the other stuff is baggage. And it reminds you that you can change the other stuff.

When I say to my mother, "I'm gonna try to get a half-hour workout after I get the kids off to school," she says, "Remember. The kids come first." I always feel guilty.

I'm raising my children with a strong Jewish identity.

I tell them they make my heart sing. They do!

Karen says that having made it through the scary part, she's not afraid of being alone. Surely, some of that confidence comes from moving up professionally and seeing that her children are well adjusted and high achievers. She puts nice dinners on the table, they get enough love and attention. However, single moms raising their children without a husband and financial security face one tough road.

We have to ask, Why did Karen's temple fail her? Why did she need to reach out to Zen Vipassana for spiritual comfort? What social, cultural, and materialistic aspects of Jewish life fail to support separated and divorced women? What price will Judaism pay for this derelict behavior?

Despite her situation, Karen doesn't complain. "I'm coping and I'm competent," she sums up.

Three days after our interview, Karen made it a point to give me an addendum. She had been thinking about our conversation and she wanted me to include this.

"When you work and raise kids, the *hardest* part is whatever choice you make, you feel guilty. It's never enough."

Wendy

WENDY, 35, is a feisty divorcée with attitude. Raised in a Reform home, she was forced to be confirmed and, after that, was done with religion. "I'm an agnostic, I don't pray."

Now a junior partner earning over a hundred thousand in a Florida law firm, and a single mom to her three-and-a-half-year-old daughter, she grew up in a wealthy suburban home, her father a surgeon, her mother a doctor's wife.

"My father's a control freak, he's used to being king and I model myself after my father. It's weird because my mother was very involved in [his] decisions."

Wendy is a tall, sun-streaked blond, wearing diamond ear-studs and a tennis bracelet. She speaks with authority. She's poised and perfectly groomed in crisp white shorts and a designer shirt.

With a B.A. in English, she worked in Manhattan for a couturier who gave weekend parties in the Hamptons, and "you could only get promoted if you were homosexual." So at twenty-four, she went to law school; it seemed intellectually challenging.

In practice nine years, her specialty is federal discrimination work in employment.

I MARRIED AT thirty. Why? I was pregnant and showing. We were living together a year and a half and made all the mistakes. I really didn't want to get married and he did. He was Irish Catholic, but my father liked him. He's a good-looking man, a personable attorney—what more could they want? We got married by a clerk, we didn't invite anybody. My mother cried. I think my dad said, "I saved twenty-five grand."

He never went to church and now he's going to church with the baby—turned into a religious person. We didn't talk about how we were going to raise children. He's eight years older than me and I was stupid and I'm paying for it now. I didn't choose my mate well, in hindsight—I'm sorting it out—because of my privileged upbringing. My dad would give me everything. I had a horse my whole life, and I brought my horse and my BMW to the university with me. Everything!

I looked for all the wrong qualities. I wanted someone really good looking, that I had to have. I never looked at a potential mate as someone who could provide for me. So I got this fabulous looking guy, he was better looking than JFK, my sister almost fell off her chair. I had everything, I didn't need anything, I looked at a guy like a new sportscar. A trophy. He was a lawyer, he could make the lingo, Irish, a raconteur, very charming. We didn't give a thought to long term and then when I got pregnant . . . Well, he shows up five months into the pregnancy with a prenuptial agreement mandating that I continue to work. The beginning and the end right there. Abominable!

At that moment I no longer loved him. Mandated the children be raised Catholic, [though] eventually he took it out.

I was tormented with this document, forty-eight pages. I signed a financial agreement, no problem, he had nothing. He probably perceived me as [wealthy]. A lot of my friends had ponies and private planes and lived in gigantic homes, tennis courts and pools. I fell out of love, nauseous. Everything I saw in him, sexually, everything, was like, "Get away from me." A shyster lawyer [did the agreement] and he paid her five thousand dollars. It frosted my ass!

I'm thirty, I couldn't do an abortion, I'm five months.

I took a five-week maternity leave and went back full time. I was nursing, I wasn't good at it. It was a nightmare, painful; I was cringing.

I hired a professional nanny; it cost a fortune, four hundred dollars to five hundred dollars a week. I paid everything. Also the mortgage on my high-rise overlooking the ocean. I couldn't sell it. And I was buying all the groceries. He paid the mortgage on the house. I was very angry. I paid for the whole birth.

He was a smooth operator, he'd tell me, "Oh, I'm going to pay." He has horrible credit and I value my credit. He had to drive a Jaguar. I don't know where the money went, I think he hid it from me. He didn't pay me for child support for a year. Any hope of rekindling what we had was killed by the financial strain on me. I said, "You're fulla shit, everything about you is fulla shit!"

I completely lost respect for him, he had no integrity.

I initiated the divorce and . . . this is embarrassing. I tried to leave once. I took the baby—she was five, six months—the nanny, the dogs, and the parrot, put them all in my car, my BMW 5 Series, a really expensive car. He called the police and stood there while I packed the car. He got down on his knees and begged, "Please stay!" So I stayed. And the cops said, "Now I've seen it all, two lawyers fighting." I left [him] two months later.

I went to my parents in Boca. By this time my apartment was sold and they supported me. He sued me for custody and he didn't get shared custody. I was making not a lot, sixty-five thousand dollars. I went to work looking like crap, balancing a full-time, demanding job and love for my child. I hired a lawyer. Cost me a fortune, no professional courtesy.

So I told the managing partner: "I can no longer work full time unless I get set up at home with a computer and start doing appellate work. I want to work at home and come in every other day." I'm living in my parents' place; they went back north. A town house with a pool, the nanny, and three dogs. And I destroyed their house, the dogs weren't trained. Without my parents I don't know what would have happened.

I had a great flexible schedule, unless a federal judge said "Be here on this date" or if I had to try a case, a pain in the ass. I never took a pay cut. [So] I speak highly of my firm because they grew with me, older guys, early sixties and they didn't know from this.

I wanted both: to be a mommy and to hold my job.

I got no alimony, zero. And no child support for a year, zero. Now he only gives me six hundred dollars a month and he gets her every other weekend. Big deal. In the past eight months, he's taken her only once, twice, and dumps her. He doesn't use his rights. Guys will fight for the right to have their children, then they don't use it. He won't get out of my life. He insinuates himself into family gatherings. He doesn't know how much I loathe him.

How did I get through it, this balancing act? I don't know, I bite my nails. I've become a really better lawyer. I threw myself into my work. I won certain cases. I've argued in front of the second highest court in the country, appelate courts that feed into the U.S. Supreme Court. And sometimes I feel like an imposter—what am I doing here? Work is thera-puetic for me. I'm absolutely more goal oriented. Now that I'm a junior partner, I ask about my equity and my insurance—questions a man would ask. And they respect that.

I was a lawyer. I had a little kid. What was I going to do? Die? She's nice, she's smart. I just went on. My family was giving me financial sup-port. I had to buy a house and they helped me with the nanny, they've been incredibly good.

My daughter loves her daddy. So it's hard to shut the door when she comes rushing out to him, "Daddy! Daddy!"

I'm pretty happy. I'm a partner, I'm doing well financially. I'm feeling in charge. The weird thing is I've become cynical about guys. I cut right to the chase and say, "It's not going to work." I'd love to marry again because he's the right guy. [But] I don't need to. Being a single mom hasn't thrown me. I love it.

Advice for single moms? You gotta get through it, maintain your emotional balance, not get depressed. I'm not through it, custody never ends. Vulnerability is a big issue in my life now. Financially, I've made arrangements so I'm not vulnerable. And I don't want to make a lot of money because he'll say she doesn't need money. Screw him. I've become tough.

Wendy and Karen, the younger of these four women, echo certain themes.

First, their marriages were damaged by *financial* problems. They were poor money managers. Too much money or not enough: disputes over money rate high in divorce.

To cope as single mothers, both sought flexibility in the workplace. As single moms raising children alone, they needed to leave the office should their child become sick. Working flexible hours or working at home is a vital component of their balancing act.

While both women would like to remarry, they are not in a hurry to replace their first husbands. They don't *need* to remarry; and when they do, they will choose more wisely.

Finally, Wendy and Karen grew enormously in their professions, gaining stature and independence, earning respect and self-confidence. Instead of sinking into despair and depression, they *focus on work* which is therapeutic and gainful. Their financial independence reduced their *vulnerability* and created a climate where they could balance work and love with less stress.

Wendy observes that some companies, among them conservative law firms, are "growing" in their sensitivities to women's issues. This can happen when women make reasonable demands. In the past, divorced and separated women, depressed about their situation, were forced to accept inflexible, anti-family policies skewed to a man's world. Today, women speak up, forcing employers to become family friendly. Some of the old boys are bending. To keep excellent employees, they *have* to bend. Still, it's a bumpier road for single moms without a partner.

According to Rutgers University Heldrich Center for Workforce Development, while 71 percent of workers are concerned about job security, nearly all (95 percent) are concerned about spending more time with their families. In the absence of daddy and his paycheck, single moms shoulder this burden alone.

Ellen Galinsky, president of the Families and Work Institute in New York, says in the February 22, 1999, *Star Ledger*, "If your work life is going well, you're more likely to have a family life that's going well. If [it's] going badly, you're more likely to take it home."

For single moms, the balance becomes more critical. Drop off the kids, get to the job, do your work, pick up the kids, get dinner on the table, homework, baths, soccer, and dance—the competing demands are overwhelming.

About 5 percent of parents employ nannies or au pairs. Less expensive arrangements are found in the eight thousand companies that offer daycare centers. In between are single moms scrounging around for adequate childcare: grandma, a neighbor, a babysitter.

Furthermore, when men divorce, their ex-wives and children can be cut out emotionally. And once they remarry, many do not maintain a close relationship with their children from a previous marriage.

Single moms, trying to strike a balance and fighting waves of guilt, often try to be supermoms in a world that grudgingly makes room for them. Arriving home, they hit the "second shift" and try to do it all perfectly.

Once upon a time, single mothers were rare. Today, they are legion. In 1979, single-moms-and-only-wage-earners numbered 3,455,000. In 1997, that figure swelled to 5,903,000. According to researchers Ellen Galinsky and James T. Bond, almost one in four (23 percent) mothers in the workforce are single parents. They are more likely to miss work than fathers, and are less eligible for coverage under the Family and Medical Leave Act because of their higher rates of part-time employment.

Given all these hardships you might ask, Why in the world would any women *deliberately* choose to be a single mother?

Celebrities like actress Sandra Bernhard tout the joys. Bernhard *kvells* over her darling Cicely. But their elegant Greenwich Village apartment, complete with nanny, is not the lifestyle of most single moms. Bernhard answers the question "Who's the daddy?" according to her mood, but in a *New York Times* interview, she adds that because of her interest in the cabala, he had to be Jewish.

The expectations of middle-class women have changed drastically since the 1970s. Wives who were smarter than their husbands were diffident and often worked *through* them. No more! Today single women can have a baby, no husband required.

In this chapter we saw that at first single moms are shaky and scared. But often they reinvent themselves and come out stronger and wiser.

Remember Nora Ephron's poignant film *This Is My Life* about Dottie Engles, a single Jewish mom raising two daughters in New York and trying to become a stand-up comedienne in Los Angeles? Juggling auditions and her children, she concludes ruefully that "kids are happy when you're there." True?

In her new book, *Ask the Children*, Galinsky dispels a lot of myths that pile on guilt. She finds that most kids feel their working moms are doing a great job. For single moms that message is welcome; it delivers a sense of relief.

The four single moms in this chapter reveal a wide range of emotions. They tell us that married or single, with husbands or alone, we are smart and capable women.

In the next chapter, you'll hear the voices of three women who *changed their goals*, for reasons other than divorce. What provoked them? Why did they revise their priorities? How did they accomplish this? What did it cost them?

9

CHANGING GOALS, RESHUFFLING PRIORITIES

ROBERTA

FRAN

MONIQUE

Sometimes women who have chosen a clear goal for themselves continue on that path for years, sure of themselves, focused, and content with who they are. Perhaps circumstances led them to assume certain scenarios for themselves. Or, on the contrary, they may have consciously designed a life to sidestep options that seemed out of their reach. In either case, they *knew* where they were headed and they stuck to the plan.

Setting their goals for education, job, marriage, money, and children, often they go along for years functioning within those boundaries. I myself never imagined that I'd wind up teaching and writing—a dream life, out of reach, I thought, to a musician's daughter from Paterson,

New Jersey. Because their lives are comfortable and bring them a level of satisfaction, some women resist change. They like what they do, they do their work well, and they have clear priorities. Quite early, they draw a picture of themselves, choose their crayons, and stay inside the lines.

Then something happens.

The priorities they established as givens, the truths they've lived by, and the identities that defined them suddenly crumble. Everything comes to a halt. Their goals change. And however successful they may be, they want to *be* and to *do* something else.

In this chapter you will hear three women tell how they reshuffled their priorities. First ROBERTA, a highly successful, six-figure dynamo who refashioned herself into a stay-at-home mom. Then FRAN, a mother of three, beseiged with illness, financial woes, and marital problems, who attempted suicide twice before she redirected herself. Last, MONIQUE, a hidden child of the holocaust, who emerged from silence to become a confident real estate entrepreneur.

These women had courage. It's so easy to stay where you are, to keep doing what you've always done, and to be what others expect. It takes guts to risk tossing it all aside and crossing over into alien territory. Roberta, Fran and Monique had the courage to change their goals.

Roberta

ROBERTA, 36, is married and the mother of a son, 3, and a daughter, 18 months. Her husband's background is "very dissimilar. My family, we're superachievers, far more intellectual and active in the community."

Her mother died after a long illness when Roberta was seventeen. Raised in a Reform home, she took solace with her friends at JFTY (Jewish Federation of Temple Youth). "But," she declares, "I'm an agnostic."

She is small and trim; dark, cropped hair, and very pretty—surprisingly laid back. We meet in a restaurant she's chosen near her home in Princeton, New Jersey.

An English major, she was "completely career- and success-driven, money and power" and became a buyer for Abraham and Strauss at age twenty-five. After seven years, she moved on to a better deal because she knew exactly where she wanted to go.

WE WERE MARRIED *only six, eight months and I decided to take a chance and move to another company in Columbus, Ohio. My husband was in advertising but he was unemployed. I was the breadwinner; his income was half of mine. In Ohio I worked a ninety- to a hundred-hour week. We had no overwhelming need to have children. It stemmed from my mother. I didn't want to leave them; it was a [real] fear.*

I slept only a few hours a night. I got tremendous satisfaction out of it. But they used techniques of humiliation to motivate us. Every Monday there was group humiliation [meetings]. I met women who should not have had children, [not] a maternal bone in their body, and they spoke poorly of their husbands. They were by far the breadwinners, [in] a position affecting a billion dollars. Hard and bitter, nasty and empty.

Well, I brought [all] that home and I became that way. [Made] comments about my husband and I went for the jugular. I was traveling 50–60 percent of the time. To Turkey, trips overseas, Hong Kong, Korea, Paris, Milan, London.

And so we developed parallel lives. The upshot was, I wasn't there, and when I was, I wasn't nice. He's an introvert, his inclination is to withdraw, not attack, to avoid confrontation. Not to sound dramatic, I decided to save myself and my marriage and we moved back East.

So now I'm making over six figures, that was my goal. I'm working outside Philly and my husband is in an agency in New York, and his salary is closing the gap between us. And I started thinking . . . There's more to life than achieving. I started seeing babies and having all those feelings. I was turning thirty. My father had remarried, a wonderful woman. They were getting older and I wanted my children to know them. It was coming back to family, family.

When my son was born, I continued to work, yes. I had a nanny. It was a tremendous conflict. She was wonderful, but I was resentful that some-one else was taking care of my baby. I couldn't, at that point, stay home, and I still loved working. And my husband hadn't achieved the next level, [so] I worked.

Here's a painful story. My son walked early, at eight months, and when he took his first steps, he walked to [the nanny], not to mommy, and I sobbed. It hurt very much. It crossed my mind that I was missing [those moments].

I was nursing, and the other issue is, he was in our bed a lot. I needed time for him. He slept in our bed most nights; he didn't use his crib too much, which binded him to me. My husband's not home till seven, seven-thirty. Sometimes he sees our son, but if he's tired I put him to sleep.

[And] of course, it's horrible for sex when your baby's in your bed. And that's really what happened. Our son is still in our bed, it's still an issue. Sex is still an issue, when to do it? It's an ongoing issue to grab those moments. And the exhaustion. We did see a therapist and her contention was exhaustion was just an excuse, and I think there's some validity.

How did I balance it all?

[Once] I was in Turkey, in Istanbul, [when] I got a call that our nanny hurt her back and wouldn't return for a while. There wasn't too much I could do. My husband had just begun a new job, and we were in a big bind. We ended up not hiring another nanny. For three months we [juggled] temporary babysitters, and I took my son on the way to work and picked him up. Which forced me to shorten my work hours.

The upshot was I liked it! The first time in my career and I didn't expect how much I liked it. Enjoying time in the car with him and coming home when it was light and making dinner for him.

That was really the beginning of the emotional need to be with him. A major sea change for me. The beginning of the end of my career. It seemed I could do my job in fewer hours. I took work home, and meetings were scheduled around the time I was there. But after three months, I got another nanny and [resumed] my hours.

When I became pregnant with my daughter, I knew I didn't want to manage those hours with two children. I'd return home around seven-

thirty and have an hour and a half with my son, that was it; he went to sleep. No way I could satisfy their needs or mine in an hour and a half. I'd never see [my children] and I couldn't live like that. So I said, "I want to stay home, it's time. I've been in retail fifteen years. I've achieved. I want a dramatic change in my life. I want to be a full-time mother and stay home."

My husband was very supportive. We had wonderful nannies, but it's not so great leaving your child with someone you don't know. I don't recall any tremendous feelings of guilt, although I imagine our son being in our bed was functioning from the guilt that I wasn't there during the day. I felt I was missing his childhood, a sadness that I wasn't his primary caregiver.

I've had many conversations and I think the career-driven women are missing everything. I think it's the ultimate joy. In the balance between work and love, the children win hands down for me. You could ask me in twenty years, and I expect to achieve again; to be forever home wouldn't satisfy me.

It actually feels great [to stay home]. Initially, I missed adult interaction, I missed the excitement of delivering product and seeing it go out the store. I missed the paychecks. I missed the money. But I love what I'm doing now.

But sometimes it's stultifying, sometimes you lack personal time, the kids need you all the time. I find that very difficult, not having the freedom. But this is so much more rewarding.

Retail, when it was good it was great. But I wasn't making a difference in people's lives. Having children was far more creative.

How did we manage financially? It was a struggle. We had financial support from my parents. Very helpful, giving with no strings attached to take the stress off. Living in Princeton with two children, it's paycheck to paycheck even with six figures. My husband got a huge increase three months before our daughter was born, so it closed the gap to some extent; but there's still a shortfall, and eating into our savings just kills me. I never had to budget. I was raised in a very upscale home.

[Religiously] I've become more observant about Jewish holidays now that I have a son. He's in a Jewish nursery school. They celebrate shabbat, he wears a kipah, he says the prayers, and brings it home. But no, I haven't changed my [agnostic] position.

I feel a sense of community I haven't felt in years. I take pleasure in knowing my children will be involved in a historical and cultural attachment to Judaism. These kids are going to know a lot more than their parents. I won't keep a kosher home. But I want my kids to marry Jews, yes.

The Jewish holidays begin at sundown and my husband's in New York and it's dark by four-thirty in the winter, so it's impossible.

My identity? My self-image? When they ask for "occupation" on a form, I leave it blank. I still have a hard time thinking of myself as a stay-at-home mother; my identity is still tied up with who I was at work.

At first, it was hard [to stay home] because I didn't have a social group. But [I've] developed friendships and next year I'll be copresident of the nursery school. So I've regained a different identity from the one I had. [I'm] a full-time mom. I have a sense of accomplishment, being home. I feel a sense of control over our lives, I feel competent in my new role. That's the word, "competent."

And my husband revels in being the breadwinner, he's the man of the family. I thought my lack of contributing financially—well, it was a hurdle in my mind. I do the bills, I do the budget. My fear [was] that it would become unequal, [the] power in his favor. That didn't occur. I'm a strong person and he has respect for what I think. And given all the financial support my family has given us, it keeps us equal. I'm not earning the paycheck, but in essence I'm still contributing through my family. I know there's far more than working and I want that balance in my life.

It was impossible to be a full-time, career-driven, successful woman and give to my family the way I wanted. The children [got] what was left over and my husband got shortchanged the most.

The woman who wants to balance love and work has to keep reshuffling her priorities. I don't foresee it changing. Women will always have the ultimate burden of balancing. It's the ultimate issue.

A few days after our interview, Roberta called me back to add these afterthoughts.

"As a Jewish woman, it's all for the children. We have an obligation to repopulate the world, to survive as Jews. Without children, you don't perpetuate the Jewish people. Without children, life is meaningless.

"I was going to be that superwoman. I was going to have it all. And now I know you can't."

Roberta's goals changed dramatically when she decided to go from being a six-figure breadwinner to a stay-at-home mom, a change made possible only with her wealthy parents' support. Few working women can do this.

Fran

FRAN, 53, is the mother of three grown children and the program director of a large Reform congregation in Florida. Unlike Roberta, whose parents were affluent, Fran battled money problems. Deeply depressed, she made two attempts at suicide. Faced with a difficult marriage, health problems, and a series of desperate part-time jobs to keep her going, she even left her husband. For six years she struggled to get her life together. Two years ago she reestablished the marriage.

Fran had no family to help her and too many stressful episodes in her life. Dashing from under one dark cloud to another, she made poor choices. Yet hers is a story of tenacity, perseverance, and triumph. A woman who ultimately succeeded by reorganizing her prioriites and changing her goals.

Fran is a heavyset woman, wearing a dressy navy pantsuit and lots of gold jewelry. She has a B.A. in community psychology and is working on a master's in Jewish studies. With a background in VISTA, the domestic Peace Corps, she married at twenty-four. She and her husband moved to Canada for eight years, living in Oakville and Hamilton, Ontario, where times were tough.

She tells her story in disjointed parts, filled with details of despair, accidents, and bad luck. Sometimes her story reaches soap opera intensity. Yet it has the ring of truth; we all know someone like her.

I MET MY *husband in Chicago at a horrible Jewish dance. We lived in the sticks and didn't even have a car. So we moved to Canada to start fresh. We were down to sixteen dollars before he got a sales job, and I found out I was pregnant. We were emergency foster parents to make extra money; we were sleeping on the floor. Our son was colicky [but] I needed to work. I [took] a temp job and left him at somebody's house. Two years later we had a daughter. We kept moving, we kept saying, "We'll start over." A lot of dumb mistakes about money, a lot of problems in the marriage.*

We bought a little house in a nice area, then we moved to another house which we ended up losing. One move was to a basement for $140 a month to save money, but we were no better off. Each time we moved, fourteen times, we hoped for a better life. I had my third child, a son. I hired a housekeeper so I could sell furniture full time, but the chain folded.

My husband had an injury to his back. A lot of misfortune, it wasn't an easy life. Issues of money and health. I developed asthma and had pneumonia. My mother and brother moved to Canada from Chicago and my mother became very despondent. So I took her on a trip to Florida and I called my husband and said, "Maybe we don't have to wait until we're sixty-five." He drove with the kids all night and he was able to find a job as a manager of a carpeting store. So we came to Coral Springs, Florida.

But when we returned to Canada to pack up, we were in a tremendous car accident which resulted in two surgeries for my husband. He was on heavy drugs, going through heavy-duty drug withdrawal. At that point, my life was in turmoil.

I decided I couldn't go on that way. I'd go back to school. I'd get my head someplace else.

*So I went to Nova University in Florida and finally got through, with
my mother's help. My husband bought a measuring business that does
floor-covering measurements for retail and department stores; they do the
blueprints and measure yardage. But my marriage was falling apart,
worse and worse. And I [got] despondent. My self-esteem plummeted.*

*On two occasions I did attempt suicide. I wasn't the mother I wanted
to be. I'm trying to give my daughter dancing lessons and I'm carting my
boys to basketball—the pretense of what a nice Jewish family is supposed
to be. I honestly thought my husband would take care of me in the traditional [way]. I thought my life would be mother and volunteering. Work
was something I was trying to avoid. My husband would be the breadwinner absolutely.*

*Both suicide attempts were in Florida. Once, when we were going to
lose our house and the children were angry. I took pills, I took over eighty
aspirins. I was brought to the hospital unconscious, they pumped my
stomach. I attempted it again just prior to leaving my husband in 1990.
We'd had a bar mitzvah, a beautiful affair. My last hurrah. I felt overwhelmed all the time, and it was not what I thought my life would be. A
lot of chaos, chaos.*

You can't do it all. Nobody does it all.

*You say [to yourself], If I'm skinny; [you say], If I had my Master's. I
always felt inadequate. Even in the house, the order and discipline was
lax. I didn't know how to manage, I wasn't a good housekeeper.*

I wanted the best for my kids. [And] I was very unfulfilled.

*[So] I left my husband and took my daughter. I went into therapy for
two and a half years and I was made the heavy, trying to make me [seem
like] the crazy lady. The two boys went with my husband. I planned this
for a month, I saved up the money to move out with my daughter to an
apartment. I worked two and three jobs at a time. I was trying to find
peace of mind.*

*Six years later my husband and I got back together. But I've never re-
gretted [that period]. It was a peaceful life we created. I was working full
time, substituting in the high school, telemarketing, whatever would bring*

in money. I was struggling tremendously with the finances. But [I was] happy that I was getting myself together.

Today our kids are grown up. We're together, though we have no sexual relationship.

My advice is: work on yourself. *In the process of working on money and raising your children, work on finding out what's real to you and not living the* oughts *and* shoulds *of the world.*

I'm selected for the Hadassah Leadership Academy, one of 150 women. It's a very exciting component of what I'm doing now. I'm getting the depth of education I want and, please God, they're paying my way to Israel next year. And the following year we go to Washington and learn about lobbying.

I feel like I'm telling you this story about someone else who is unconnected to the person you see in front of you. Who am I now? Very positive about my environment. I have options.

A Jewish *phenomenon is that we have expectations for education, for money, and for the good life that everyone else wants. And we work really hard on it. I think it's to the good, some of this aggressiveness and go-after-it.* What changed me is CAJE [*Central Agency for Jewish Education*]. *The best of the best were there, authors of textbooks. [It] showed me my Jewish education was very limited. I started taking classes; [I saw] a lot of opportunities.*

I think I'm in a good place. I feel appreciated. I love my job, I'm able to be creative and bring Judaism into lives on a daily basis. My husband is doing, thank God, fine, his health problems are over. And our children are doing well. My husband is proud of me and now we're communicating. I'm not just house *oriented or* appearance *oriented. I was [once] frantic about* looking *nice. Now I'm* feeling *nice. And out of the chaos came three kids who are mensches.*

Unlike Roberta, Fran's goal was not to work. She expected to be taken care of; Roberta's goal was to achieve a six-figure career. Then she had children and changed. Both women did an about-face. Each changed her goals and reorganized her priorities. Each learned to tune into what she really wanted, not what she thought she should want. For Roberta, the struggle to change her priorities was eased by her family's financial support. For Fran, the stuggle was aggravated by poor health, poor choices, and downright despair. Nevertheless, Fran emerged from the chaos with a job she loves. She became a working woman appreciated by her husband. Fran became positive and optimistic.

Monique

MONIQUE, 64, has two adult daughters and one grandson. Born in Paris, she survived the Nazi occupation of France. Like an Audrey Hepburn gamin, she is that ageless Parisian with a French accent and auburn, bobbed hair. Under her laugh lines, a pixie peeks out.

One of the Hidden Children interviewed by Steven Speilberg, she lived with Catholic nuns for six months. "Our parents put us in hiding in a convent, put us under a different name. I know the catechism, yes."

She remembers how her family fled the Nazis from the time she was five until she was ten, and how her father uprooted them and brought them to the south of France. "Things were very bad for the Jews. We were so afraid to be stopped at the borders and my father was on guard all night." She remembers how her little sister wept. "She cried constantly, constantly, and I felt responsible for her."

Monique received her degree in kindergarten teaching at the College Sevigne in Paris, and she has had many careers: teacher, real estate manager, and entrepreneur.

Today she lives in Highland Park, a suburb of Chicago, and though she has sold her import business, she continues to work with her lawyer husband and to live a Jewish life.

"We were in hiding a long time during the war, we didn't have much of a Jewish life. Now I keep a kosher home, not *strictly* kosher.

But we don't work on *shabbos* and we observe all the holidays." Monique describes herself as "very Jewish conscious."

THE FIRST TWO *years of our marriage, we lived in Israel and I worked full time as a teacher. It takes a lot out of you. So when my first daughter was born, I realized with a little child you just stay home. In those days my mother-in-law was a very powerful, hard-working woman, and my husband expected me to work like his mother. For me it was culture shock because my father never permitted my mother to work.*

When we got back to the United States, I thought I'd teach Montessori because I was educated by one of the students of Madame Montessori. But by that time, my husband was doing well and we didn't need the money, so it was easier to have a more simple life than making more money and spending more money. Everyone had two cars; we had one, a used car. We arranged it so I could stay home. It was a choice, not a sacrifice, oh no, no, no, I enjoyed every minute of it!

And then we bought a home. That was my dream and I was very happy. I wanted to be the housewife. When my second daughter was born — nine months after the snowstorm! — I was busy helping my husband, entertaining his lawyers. Not in a fancy way, no, in a very French way, simple. It was always a plus, and any big deals were done in the house. To this day I coordinate everything.

Through his law firm, my husband came across a building. Twenty-eight apartments in Evanston, a very fine neighborhood. We bought it and rented apartments to Northwestern University students. One apartment was so horrible, I could not see myself asking someone to clean the toilet. So I put on long gloves and did it myself.

I started out looking for furniture. Then I found a concierge — do you say "superintendent"? He and his wife were from Belgium, French-speaking, and they loved my children and they became my sitters. I learned the business and how to speak English, not perfect but very good. And I managed all twenty-eight apartments. For Christmas I used to send chocolates. And when the heat broke down, I rented heaters for everyone. I made a nice laundry room and we put up posters; the children did it with me. I learned bookkeeping and somehow I built it so well that two years later we sold it for four times the price.

Afer that, I retired for one week.

My next career happened by accident. Some Israeli friends needed advice. It had to do with quality control equipment that measures the thickness of tin and tin alloy that bonds to steel. The steel is used to make cans for food—a can of sardines, a can of soup. They were a very small company, they sold one, two machines, and suddenly they got an order for thirty machines from American Can, which was located a few miles away from us.

My husband was the lawyer, he arranged the final deal, and when the machines arrived I went there and looked at them and I learned a little bit about it. Meanwhile, our Israeli friends asked me to be their distributor for the U.S. so I went back to American Can. I didn't know anything, but I had physics and chemistry and geography because the French high schools are very advanced, and I knew the map.

They said, "We'll help you." And they did!

They introduced me to the top people in the steel mills, who sell to the can manufacturers, who sell to the canners. They got me to the very top of U.S. Steel and Bethlehem Steel. It was unbelievable, unbelievable! I had trade shows to do, I had to travel and my husband gave me a little corner of his office with a part of his secretary, the part nobody else wanted. I learned it all on my own.

I was such a shy little girl, but I was enterprising.

Maybe because I was a hidden child. You learn a lot about what is to be hidden, you hide yourself completely and suddenly you come out of your shell. You know there are things you can do and you're not afraid anymore. When I joined the group of hidden children, I started learning this. And when I went to Israel the first time, I saw people dancing in the street. I felt free, I was out of hiding. I spoke loudly. It changed my life completely.

After the war, I remember my family name was Dreyfus. In history class we had to study the Dreyfus Affair, and I made myself so sick, I got myself a temperature so I wouldn't have to go to school. I went home. It was so embarrassing that someone would point a finger and say I was Jewish. I was miserable. And once the teacher pointed at me; I must have been seven. Her name was Madame Cassat. I had jet black hair and she would walk down the aisle to look for lice, you got it from the trains and the soldiers. The other children, not being Jewish, had lighter color hair. Everyone had lice and my mother had removed the eggs with vinegar. But the teacher pointed me out to another teacher in the playground: "Look, the girl with lice." They called me "the foreigner." This was the occupied zone of France, when we lived south of Paris, far away in Brive.

My mother was doing everything for us so we could survive. I saw her making soap with caustic acid and she would cry and turn her head. All the things she had to invent for us. So to me, housewife was a tremendous profession, one of surviving. I like the feeling of home.

And nowadays I love Friday night. I dress up in a pretty dress. I always have company. You sit there, you have a beautiful table, a bunch of flowers. I love beauty. I get a lot of pleasure from a little flower. So to me, preparing Friday night is a reward for the week of work.

But there were trade-offs while I was balancing my work and the family. When I had to go on trade shows—well, we all have this problem of separation. My youngest daughter, when I went away, I was paged all the time. She was hysterical and I had to come home. It was a big mistake, she needed me more. But I loved what I was doing, it was very challenging, it made me feel important. And it was very flattering to be with a lot of men who think you're wonderful. It did a lot for my ego, because I was the center of attention.

They used to joke that "Monique can be be washing the dishes and sell a forty thousand dollars machine at the same time." I did most everything on the phone. It lasted eight years. And when I went to sell my company, well . . . my husband said, "If you get ten, fifteen thousand, that'll be nice."

I went in and said, "I need forty-, uh, nine!" And that's what I got. Deal! I invested this money and did well.

But there is something else.

When my mother died, she left me a little money. Enough to say I can stand up, and it made me feel independent. When women work, they have this feeling of independence. For example, when my daughter got married, my husband was against this wedding and the first time in my life I stood up and I made the wedding [myself] because I knew it was right. This was a gift [from] my mother, she saved all her life. I invested it well and I made the wedding.

So, if at all possible, it is extremely important for women to be financially independent. I know women who live very well, a luxurious life, but they don't have a penny to their name. Without money, a woman has no power. Unless she's gorgeous, and that fades too.

After I sold the business, well, my daughter had Crohn's disease and that was a full-time job. In those days she was in school in Madison, Wisconsin, and if she called me, I'd drive all night in a snowstorm and stay there a week, two weeks. Then two years ago, she got very sick and I spent most of the year with her. At twenty-seven, twenty-eight . . . well, it was a full time job.

With Jewish women, it's not just the mother-daughter thing, we're more caring. Jews help each other, it's part of our tradition. We are a people, we are responsible for each other. With Israel, I cry when I go and I cry when I leave. Ten, twelve times.

Many women go to work because it makes them feel better and they miss out with their children. I still have a certain guilt about being away when my daughter was so miserable about being separated. Women should be paid for staying home. In France, after the war, they wanted women to produce children because we lost so much during the war. You received an amount of money for being "a woman at home." It recognized the fact that women are doing a job, their work is important. Absolutely.

But I understand women who work for the career, for the advancement. I did that. Today what is lost is a woman can't stay home to raise her children. And nobody else can do it. Not a nanny, not an au pair, nobody.

I think bringing up children and enjoying those times—unless you can't afford it—those are extremely important years in the life of children.

From a shy litle girl and a hidden child raised by Catholic nuns, Monique emerged to become a successful entrepreneur and savvy businesswoman. What was the catalyst that brought about this change? What provoked this woman with no business background and no experience to go to trade shows and take on negotiations with major moguls at Bethlehem Steel and U.S. Steel?

"You know there are things you can do and you're not afraid anymore." Monique changed her character from shy to enterprising; "I spoke loudly, I changed my life completely." Another turning point came when she stood up to her husband and made her daughter's wedding. From this experience of power, she concludes that "it is extremely important for women to be financially independent."

Fran learned this, too. Her job gave her financial independence and with it came her husband's respect. When Fran changed her priorities from *looking* good to *feeling* good, she became "very positive," a woman with options.

Each woman in this chapter learned the power of money.

Roberta feared that staying home would reduce her power in her husband's favor. When her parents filled in the gap in their financial short-fall, she viewed it as *her* contribution and *her* money. It gave her permission to change her goals.

Indeed, balancing work and love may hinge on *who* is bringing money home. Working women are leveling the playing field and changing their priorities. A woman with no money of her own is one with reduced options.

Many women are learning to switch goals as their needs change. Children go off to school and the part-time job that once seemed so challenging now seems tame. Some decide to pursue more education; some take better jobs. Their priorities change. Paradoxically, working women know that money isn't everything. And because the nature of work is changing, goals and priorities will change too.

Each woman in this chapter changed her goals.

She rejected the life she was living *in opposition to who she really was* and she tapped into a truer version of herself.

In the next chapter, you will meet two women who are struggling to reach a decision about a *career conflict*. Their focus is work: how to find meaning in the workplace.

10

CAREER CONFLICTS, WOMEN ON THE CUSP

RIMA

DEBBI

When women entered the workforce, we began to experience some of the same problems as men. We worked in the same offices. We shared many of the same issues about salary, promotions, achievement, recognition, and bosses. Some of us came to question the very nature of our jobs. We began to ask ourselves serious questions: Is the job delivering the satisfaction we expected? Is this the job we really want?

In this chapter you will hear the voices of two successful women doing some serious soul-searching about the value of work. By chance, both are from California and both are facing a career crisis. If you think "California" means Valley girls, Hollywood moguls, and Silicon Valley millionaires, meet RIMA and DEBBI. Both are teetering on the cusp and reexamining their worklife.

Rima

RIMA, 48, could be stretched out on a chaise under the California sun checking out her cuticles. Married to a dealmaker for the Disney Channel, she rubs elbows with media people, goes to the parties, and travels widely. Her husband, an attorney, is head of business affairs. She has a house in ritzy Beverly Hills. "It's a little house," she tells me with a modest smile.

She is down-to-earth and willing to let me hear her think out loud as she ponders her earnest struggle about a career change. She speaks slowly, hesitant to make sweeping generalities.

She is a pretty woman, easy going, with good bones and tousled brown hair, dressed in a simple pair of Gap shorts and a white T-shirt. Her baby blues shine with goodwill. She has worked twenty years with adolescents facing cancer, raised two children (now grown), and earned a Ph.D. along the way. She wrote her thesis on different coping strategies of adolescents facing cancer. This is her work; a depressing occupation, some might say, but for her a grand opportunity. A commitment. A passion.

Now Rima is in a bind. She is thinking about steering her ship in another direction. But she can't decide whether to sail into the wind, take a rudderless route, or jump ship and head for shore.

I WAS RAISED in a Conservative Jewish home, no bat mitzvah, but confirmed. A clear message definitely was, you don't date non-Jewish boys. So I rebelled, I was a child of the sixties. And I got fairly serious with a non-Jewish boy my first year in college in Boston.

My parents were very upset. The guy broke up with me and my father saw this as an opportunity. He sent me to Israel. I was nineteen and I went along passively.

I met my husband on a kibbutz. He [came from] L.A. I went back to school on the East Coast and a year later we got married. I finished my undergraduate degree in California. I was nine months pregnant when I graduated!

When my son was two, I knew I needed to do something. I was twenty-five and I didn't know what I wanted to do, but I couldn't imagine being a stay-at-home mom. [By now], my husband is a lawyer making not a lot, but we had enough. He was teaching at UCLA law school.

I felt work was in the future, but what I wanted to do was go back to school. It was [about] what I wanted to do with my life. I knew I had to do something besides just be a mom.

Why is it not enough? My mother was a great role model. She seemed to be able to do everything at home and she could work. She's a marriage counselor. I didn't feel guilty. I knew I had to find something fulfilling. It was doable.

Someone told me about this gerontology program at USC, it was just opening. So I took my son in his stroller. It was May. I got an application for September and I got in on the ground floor.

There was foreign student housing and I found an Indian woman, and I'd drop him off before class and pick him up. He came home smelling like curry—he says he remembers it.

What happened is for my field placement I was [sent] to Jewish Family Services and my supervisor said, "If you're going into this work you really need to get your degree in social work."

I was very fortunate because [a friend] helped me get into the dual-degree program, social work and gerontology. I was in school three years. I found a woman who had childcare in her house. At times I felt guilty, yes. But I felt Mary's Place was a wonderful environment. It wasn't every day, it was a few hours a day and I always had time with my children.

It was a choice. I never wanted a full-time job, I never felt stretched. When I look back, all of these were choices because I never had to work. Everything down the line was a choice. I felt privileged. [Which is] a double-edged sword. Because it's a choice, there's more guilt because you could choose to stay home. You're doing it for yourself. All of it.

Why? Because I needed the stimulation, the identity, the self-worth. It's nice to make a little money. I could spend a little bit, it gave me more leeway. And my husband was very supportive, he never discouraged me. It wasn't a struggle then.

The irony of all this is that I'm struggling with this now.

Why? I'm an empty-nester. So why now, *[when] I have no kids at home? Before there was no struggle and now I'm struggling. It's a conflict. I feel I should be doing more. [But] I don't* know *what I want.*

Maybe I'm a bit burned out. Maybe I need [more challenges] on my job. What I need is more! *I feel on one hand I want to take more of an independent leadership role. And even though on paper it looks that way, in a medical environment like the hospital . . . well, I don't know if I'm clear [on this]. I'm struggling with it.*

I'm feeling more adventuresome. Maybe I should really take a risk. [Quit and] go out and start a business. Something on my own. Taking it to a different level. It's really me. *I've got to do something* independent. *It clicks—you're on your own, no kids at home. You have to go out and do something, there's a push to do* more. *And whatever that more is, I've got to find out.*

I got a lot of rewards from my job. Pleasure. Satisfaction. But I've done it for twenty years! Always worked within the confines of an institution which limited my power. Now that the kids have left, it's sparked this. Now I'm free, it's [about] my power. A psychological freedom.

How did I get to this point?

Eleven years ago, I thought about how adolescents struggle facing cancer. It's such a difficult time anyhow. Children's Hospital serves the inner city, mostly Hispanics. I've got a team of four wonderful colleagues and we started this program. It was a dream. My passion. To start a group for adolescents with cancer.

We got funding and put it together. We have support group meetings and I have a co-facilitator. We grew tremendously! We started going on retreats twice a year, where we take anywhere from forty to seventy teenagers for three days with adult chaperones. We organize a whole program.

Not only do we have fun, [there's] a mental health component to it. We train teams. We have discussions. We do training for peer counseling programs.

My husband was with me all through this. Sometimes he came and took care of the kids. He would coach the baseball team. He'd say: "Because of you, I'm going to get into heaven. Because of the work you do."

The impact on my kids? For my son, it wasn't so drastic. But my daughter was only eight. I got emotionally involved. It's weekends, too, and I think it took away from my family, because she wrote [about] it on her college essay. About how she had to wait for me after school to be picked up, all the kids leaving and her feelings of being left behind. She was upset and angry, negative feelings. But later on she talked in her essay about how proud she was of me for [my work] with children with cancer and how I was such a role model for her.

Another major drain on my family was when I was both working and involved in my doctorate. It was on different coping strategies of adolescents [facing] cancer. Many of these kids are long-term survivors. That took care of weekends, too. Going to school drained me. The Ph.D. was a high price to pay. It took me nine years to get it!

Are Jewish women [balancing work and families] different?

The stereotype is they want to be taken care of—obsessed with clothing and jewelry and materialism. What I see at work is that a lot of non-Jewish women have to work, there's no choice. Having a husband who can support me, I never play up what I have. I don't want people to be envious.

I'd say Jewish women want to grow, [we're] always striving to learn more. We put an enormous value on education. I didn't get the verbal message that I had to work. [But] observing my mom, I saw it worked for her.

Are Jewish women more attached to their mothers? Yes, all my friends are Jewish and they're all very attached to their parental families. It's not a burden. Family is very important as a value, there's still the connection.

I work at Children's Hospital with many ethnic backgrounds, and I'd say it's true for them too, Hispanics and Afro-Americans. My mother wouldn't place a value judgment on any *choice I make. My father, yes! He's controlling. Yes, [Jewish women] are very attached to their parents.*

I'd like to know what my kids think about how I balanced work and [my family]. I tried to always be there for the important things, I really tried to do both. I'd call in if I had to be somewhere, and flexibility was more important than money. As a part timer, I could exchange hours.

Advice? I liked *part time.* I liked *the way I did it. It's nice to be able to do something for yourself and be there for your kids. Nice to have both. If I didn't have the option, that's a different story. But I feel I did it right.*

It's hard to establish yourself when [your] kids have grown. [So] I feel great that I did it early on and I never dropped out of the work-place. I never missed the plays and the games. The flexibility of part time is important. I was content to be part time. The family always came first.

Now *[with the kids gone] part of the struggle is I'll never know what I'm worth [if] I don't challenge myself. If I don't do something very inde-pendently, take something on. I'm thinking about a couple of things.*

What are they?

Private practice, *which is horrible out there. The field of adolescence is still a passion. Do I want to go on my own? I always had the security of an institution. Children's Hospital is a prestigious institution to have be-hind you [for] twenty years.*

Or maybe something more *entrepreneurial. Something to do with travel. Like taking developmentally disabled teenagers on a travel pro-gram, giving them an opportunity they'd never have, with a psycho-social component to it. Teens with those problems don't have [travel]. Indepen-dence and autonomy is a big issue [for them]. You'd have to have a phy-sician and a nurse [along].*

Another thing is teaching *at the university level. Develop a social work minor. Teach two classes and develop an internship program. It's a little scary [but] I like working with students, it's worth exploring. I'd have to develop a syllabus.*

Another hairy option—and my husband tells me this—is to take time off and just enjoy. I do clay sculptures and I could take a course and pursue art classes.

That's the problem. I have too much on my plate!

One thing [I'd like to add] is the relationship with your spouse. My husband and I are very focused on work and the one thing we didn't do was [give] more time for ourselves. We have a good social life, but we don't go away by ourselves. Spend more time with [your] husband!

As Rima ponders her midcareer dilemma, are you wondering why a successful woman with a Ph.D. would be conflicted at the twenty-year mark? It appears that, like men at midcareer, Rima is asking about the very value of her work. An important question. An existential question. And one that demands a pragmatic decision.

What is the true worth of my work? Should I continue? Jump ship? Redirect myself? If work defines us, *who am I?*

At midcareer, Rima feels the need "to grow" and to challenge her powers. There is something deeply metaphysical in this inquiry. It is not merely about work, it is about *meaning* in one's work. Perhaps it takes twenty years in the workplace to arrive at that point. Women who are serious about their work are likely to confront this issue.

Fortunately, Rima has many options. Drop out of the workforce and take art lessons? Teach at the university level? Become an entrepreneur and set up travel programs for developmentally disabled teenagers? Or open a private clinical practice? She can earnestly examine her options; her back is not against the wall.

Several months after this interview took place, I learned her decision. Of the four choices she outlined, which do you think Rima chose?

She took the teaching job. And she's having a great time doing two graduate-level courses at a university in Malibu.

A step down? I don't think so.

Like Rima, women raising small children may choose to cut back when their children are young and they are juggling the demands of family life. Elizabeth Gelfand, Universal studio vice president of marketing strategy and an eleven-year studio veteran, told the *Hollywood Reporter*, in a special issue on women in entertainment, that after she marketed *Jurassic Park*, a very intense time, she decided juggling with a new baby was unfair to everybody and went part time. Producer Wendy Finnerman, mother of three, who did *Forrest Gump* and *Stepmom*, also went part time, because "It's family first, work second, and I fit in who knows where." These women fashioned their work around their families *while the kids were small*.

However, once this phase of a woman's life passes, she may hit the same existential crisis Rima confronted when she became an empty-nester. Women committed to work may *sequence in and out* of the workforce while raising kids. But the value of work itself can change drastically at midlife. Later, when their kids are grown, they may stop to ask themselves hard questions. Is their current job feeding their soul? Is the job what they really want to do for the rest of their life?

Debbi

DEBBI, 36, a "thank you very much" in-charge woman with streaked blond hair, is close to six feet tall and reed thin at 112 pounds. She is flamboyant in that Rodeo Drive way that spells "confident and rich." Quite used to getting things done her way.

Debbi is also at a career impasse.

We meet at the posh hotel suite where she is staying. Her two daughters, 11 and 6, are enjoying room service and watching TV in the adjoining bedroom and she introduces me. They could be an elegant mother-daughters photo out of *Town and Country*.

Pouring tea from a fine china pot, she tells me she does the financials for her husband part time. But she's quick to add that she gave up a glorious career as a Julliard-trained singer and worked full time with Columbia Pictures in New York as an international marketer for television and theatricals. She also has an M.B.A. from Columbia University. "Too many Columbias in my life," she remarks.

Seven and a half years ago, the family packed up and moved from New York to San Francisco.

Debbi is a woman on the cusp of a life change which she is eager to explain to me. She is a fast, showy talker and she interrupts herself to give asides, opinions, and declarations.

"I've come full circle," she states as I set up the tape recorder. I detect a level of frustration, which she wants me to validate.

Debbi is a woman poised on the high board, ready to dive. To take on a new career or pick up the career she relinquished to help her husband.

I CAME FROM *a conflicted, observant home. My father followed the dogma. My mother is from Argentina, she was not observant, she was Zionistic and militant. But Jews to the tips of their toes. For a skinny model, she was very involved, had a degree in math, and she was Miss Argentina in the late fifties. Our house was* glatt kosher *[very strict] and the maids couldn't keep it straight. Her favorite sandwich was BLT. Very conflicted. A constant battle.*

At thirteen, I was outspoken and I walked away from a gorgeous bat mitzvah to [conclude] that religion was a crock. My father was a dentist, we had nice things, we traveled all over the world: Europe, the Caribbean, South America. We had maids, yes, and we lived in Westchester [County, New York].

I married at twenty-five. My daughter was born a year and a half later and we joined the Sutton Place Synagogue, a very, very *wealthy congregation. Gifts started at $250,000. A lot of snobbishness. I quit over [an incident] when my daughter was not allowed in the sanctuary. I thought the rabbi was a hypocrite. I never,* ever, *questioned my identity as a Jew, but I certainly questioned organized religion.*

Ultimately, we enrolled at the Park Avenue Synagogue, which was magnificent. I looked for a place where there was meaning in Jewishness.

I've come to realize that what's important for me is the sense of commu-nity and belonging. Now [in California] we belong to a very Conserva-tive congregation, Beth Shalom.

My work life? I was a singer, educated at Julliard. I performed all over the place. I started on keyboard, piano, organ when I was three. Violin by eight. Julliard at twelve. And I studied with the most wonderful teachers and coaches all through high school. I did touring companies of Broad-way shows, I did regional, I did summer stock. Fantastics, My Fair Lady, Bye Bye Birdie, Grease. I was fifteen, sixteen, seventeen; a professional, getting paid. I made lots of money and joined the union.

When it was time to go to college, I decided on a broader education than just sticking with a conservatory. It's wonderful, but a very stifling environment, very political, a lot of competition among the teachers [about] who's singing what. I was a straight-A student going to high school full time while I was doing all this, [and] I thought I should have a real education.

I chose Columbia so I could continue with my teacher and my coach, and I ended up doing a double major in music and history, with a minor in economics. I was singing mostly classical repertoire, planning to go to Europe.

[But] my father had a heart attack. And two voice lessons a week at a hundred something a pop, plus the coaching at $150 a session, was cost-ing a fortune. It was a real eye-opener for me. [But] I'm a nice Jewish girl, I don't want to wait tables. I believe in beshert. *[So] I apply to Har-vard Business School and I get in. It scared the shit out of me and I de-cided [to wait] and got a job in a small consulting firm. I spoke Italian, French, and Spanish well and I could get by in German. I had a great time for two years as a research analyst. Then I met my husband, got ac-cepted to Columbia Business School, and got married at the end of the first semester.*

It was just unheard of! Barnard women didn't do that! It was a mili-tant, feminist, career-oriented school. You got your Ph.D., you traveled. You didn't marry and have children.

[Anyhow], it was the worst recession in New York. My husband was

doing hostile takeovers. New York was a depressing place, it looked like the city would never come back. He was in the process of buying a company in San Francisco, commuting. [So] we moved, we just did it. We called it the Great Escape.

I thought [California] would be fun. Any time I wanted to do something, [I did it]. I wanted to sing, I sang. I wanted Julliard, I went. There's nothing in my life that's not doable. I set my mind to it, I work my ass off, and I get it done.

[Back] in New York, I was working for my husband. In what capacity? Every capacity. Doing his financial analysis, doing his marketing and investor relations. He had been partners with a big raider, a takeover guy, and he left the firm and said, "I'm going on my own and who's going to answer the phone? I'm going to launch my own hostile takeover!" And I said "Okay." Our daughter was eight months old. Nine-to-five would have been my dream. I was there fifteen hours a day!

How did I do it? Balance work and love?

It was awful! After all those years of professional training and all that money, I got lost in the shuffle. I loved my child, [but] I wanted to work. I don't have a lot of respect for women who don't work. My mother ran my father's [dental] practice, she worked like a lunatic, made dinner, and went back to work. But with me, it was terrible.

There's this child I love. And I have to tell you I don't get on the floor and do baby play. I don't go to the park. I don't do zoos. But I love my kids as people. And I was unbelievably torn. I felt guilty.

And the worst was, [my husband] was way too young to have kids, way too young to be married. He was twenty-eight when we had a baby, he wasn't ready. [And] he's got a wife, a child, the pressures of business, tuition, an apartment on the Upper East Side. It was a fucking nightmare! The pressures of New York in the late eighties, I can't describe it.

One day the baby's sick. The housekeeper calls me, she's got 102 temperature. I'm in the office and my child is having trouble breathing. So I said to my husband, "I gotta go." And he said, "You're not leaving, you have stuff to do."

Our family income, before he went on his own, was in excess of one, *two million dollars. [But] we took a big hit in the stock market in '89 and we went from him having a partnership draw and a percentage of every deal to just owning this company. It was tremendous stress.*

How do you balance being a wife, an employee, a mother, and being me? You don't! You say, "Enough"; you say, "Enough!" You quit cold turkey.

[So now] we're out there in San Francisco. And I said, "My job for the next year is trying to get this family settled, and making sure my kid is sane and stable and she's happy in her school, and putting a house and a life together." He didn't need me anymore, he had hired people—and the tension of being together, it didn't work for us.

We come from different backgrounds. His world revolves around him. *He came from a family where it was all about show. You basically looked out for yourself. Everything was materialistic. Appearance.*

So working together, for us, was terrible. [So] in San Francisco I said, "Enough!" I decided, It's time to stop. It's time for me to get sane.

He was thrilled *to have me gone. He couldn't stand it. The problem was we were together twenty-four hours a day. I didn't want to fight with him at the office because then I had to go home and he carries a grudge. So the pressure was terrible. I lost a ton of weight.*

Well, the year to get my life in order turned into four years. So now our second child is born and I really had an excuse to be home. Am I enjoying it? No, no! It felt wrong, it didn't feel like me. To be home, to be driving carpools with these women who play tennis, to go to the supermarket. It revolted me. But I couldn't figure out another way to do it. I have two kids, and the lessons and the tutors and the Hebrew school and the driving. I felt the kids needed me. I couldn't figure out what I wanted for myself. I knew I wanted to be working. I knew I wanted to be a good mother to my kids. I knew my husband was traveling all the time and the only way to keep the family was to travel all together. The marriage wouldn't survive if we didn't stay as a unit.

[But] I have an M.B.A. I'm a musician. To go back to performing by definition means [being] on the road. I thought about teaching. But [then] my father got pancreatic cancer [and died]. And it destroyed my

daughter. *He was the only constant male in her life, he was her father. Even in San Francisco, he saw her every two weeks, he did her math homework over the phone. My husband? [He's] working, involved in exercise and his life. He does yoga six days a week.*

Where is Debbi? Nowhere.

Now, finally, I'm figuring it out. I can be doing things for myself. The only answer I have is, life is about phases. What doesn't work is trying to pile it all on at the same time.

I'm really lucky. I had a rich career as a teenager and young adult because of the music. I had a fabulous education. I got to work for [Columbia Pictures] and a consulting firm. I got to travel all over the place.

I'd like to go back to performing. To do something glamorous, exciting, and lucrative. To have a life!

Debbi gave up her career to work in her husband's business. Like many women trapped in mama-poppa businesses, she spent the entire day with her spouse. This intensified the tension when her husband carried a grudge home with him or demanded she stay at work when their child was ill.

Women who have toiled in a family business know that scenario. Indeed, immigrant women often worked alongside their mates because the family could not have survived otherwise. But this is not the case for Debbi, whose husband made millions. Clearly, she feels that after all those years of professional training and all that money she "got lost in the shuffle."

Debbi is grieving for a lost self and for a career she gave up. Conflicted and confused, she is teetering on the cusp, hoping she can return to work that is "glamorous" and "exciting." As a Julliard-trained musician and a woman who speaks three languages fluently, she has marketable skills.

Debbi is facing a painful truth, that work chosen because it seems the right *family* decision can become a rock on your chest. When we sacrifice work that we love, we excise a part of ourselves. As Jewish working women, how much sacrifice is required? And for how long can we deny who we are and what our work means to us?

Detractors may argue that Debbi wants to be taken care of in style, and that wailing "I wannabe a star" is unseemly. Still, Debbi's story addresses the pain caused when a career conflict arises *well before midlife*, when the job simply doesn't deliver satisfaction. As a Jewish woman, Debbi, like her mother, was instructed to sacrifice for her family. Debbi follows this role model until it backfires and she says, "Enough!"

Today Jewish working women, reared for a life in the workplace, are questioning the value of their work. Being Jewish, you're supposed to be the best at *everything*. Good mother. Terrific wife. Dutiful daughter. Best on the job. At some point these messages collide. Debbi is feeling that pain.

Many working women are switching careers in their thirties, forties and fifties. Like Rima and Debbi, they are taking a personal inventory of their strengths and weaknesses. In an effort to nurture their soul, they struggle through a period of introspection and confusion. In this chapter you heard the voices of two women on the cusp of career changes.

In the next chapter, you will hear two women who resolved conflicts and came out on the other side of the tunnel. Women with strong feelings about *assimilation and feminism*.

11

ASSIMILATION,
FEMINISM

NATASHA

JOAN

Many Jews express concern about assimilation and feminism. They believe these two social forces are to blame for sapping the spiritual strength of Judiasm. They view assimilation and feminism as twin evils destroying Jewish families and eroding the essence of our faith.

In this chapter you will meet two women who belie these fears. An ardent feminist who wanted no children and now enjoys a family with deep connections and commitments to Judaism. A Russian immigrant who was ashamed to be called a Jew and now has found her roots through assimilation. Neither feminism nor assimilation impeded their attachment to Judaism. They have created Jewish homes enriched by Jewish values.

It has taken some Jews a century to shed their status as immigrants. To become "real Americans" was what our grandparents and great-grandparents sought with fervor. Many studied at night school to learn to write and speak English "vidout-hen-exsen." To become a citizen and be able to vote in an American election were highly prized gifts to those whose lives were scarred by vicious pogroms, government massacres, and virulent anti-Semitism. The second wave of immigrants came to our shores later, victims of the Holocaust.

Arriving in America, the land of the free, most immigrants sought to assimilate. What could prove they belonged more than active participation in American life? Freedom to speak out without fear of reprisal captured their imagination. So they wrote, they composed, they invented. They were free! Each wave of immigration produced its own leaders in politics, film, music, art, science, and medicine.

Soon first- and second-generation Jewish women also rose to positions of leadership. Today Bette Midler and Barbara Walters are household names, and every American knows our beloved diva and superstar, Barbra Streisand. *Jewish Women in America* lists a mind-boggling eight hundred biographies of women whose contributions are astonishing.

In the early twentieth century, my Russian grandfather Joseph Grudin was thrown in jail for his political beliefs. The Grudins (then Grudsky) immigrated to America to make a better life. My father Maurice was born in Hoboken, New Jersey, and grandpa joined the Workman's Circle and became a labor advocate. My grandmother Rachel, observing that her Maichele (my father) was a gifted pianist at six, purchased an ebony concert Mason and Hamlin grand piano used by the Metropolitan Opera, and she paid it off over many years. *Jews had to give their children every advantage. America was the land of opportunity.*

Today, Jews are still trying to give their children every opportunity. A century of assimilation has whittled us into "valid Americans," and many of us are so secularized that some rabbis beseech us not to neglect our Jewish roots, and to return to our spiritual covenant with God. Are Jewish families Jewish enough?

Today Jewish families are divorced, intermarried, single parented, and blended—situations that were once rare. The reality is that most Jews are becoming less observant and less religious. Even Orthodox Jewish wives, trained to be modest and dutiful, are now suing abusive husbands. Who can resist the powerful forces of American culture with its insistence on individual rights?

Becoming more American, we became less Jewish. Assimilation was the process.

For NATASHA, however, assimilation produced the reverse. Ashamed to be labeled a Jew in Kiev, Natasha's immigration to America produced more than a journey, it produced a spiritual rebirth. For her, assimilation actually resulted in her reattachment to Judaism. Like my grandmother Rachel, she yearned to give her son opportunities. Today, Cubans and Mexicans, Asians and Koreans, Indians and Haitians all come to America seeking the same opportunities.

Natasha

NATASHA, 49, a computer programmer, greets me at the front door of her split-level home in a velvet robe and slippers. It is a cold December night and she is home from work, relaxing. With her huge almond eyes and high cheekbones, she has the chiseled good looks of an actress.

"Wait, wait," she spreads a kitchen towel to protect her marble dining room table before I can set down my tape recorder.

Natasha tells us how she made the decision to escape to America. She speaks with a Russian accent and from the heart. Her eyes well up, her gestures say what words can not express.

IN 1980 I came here from Russia. Why? The reason was Russia. The situation politically was very difficult. Russia provoked me to leave Russia. I was a Russian Jew and there was no life there, no future. I was thirty years old, I had a little boy asking questions and it was a very good situation to get out.

My boy was asking me "What is a Jew?" because he was called "kike" in his kindergarten. "What's wrong with me?" He was six, seven years old. I felt obligated to take my son out of the country. My husband and

I felt it was the right time. And it was. Because a year later, they closed the borders.

Back then, in order to get anywhere, you had to be ten times smarter and work twenty times harder than anybody else. And that's what we did. I lived in Kiev, it was very anti-Semitic. Ukraine is very anti-Semitic. That was the political situation.

It's funny. My degree was in mechanical engineering and my husband was a school teacher of physical education. Both of us got our degrees and nice jobs, but we couldn't survive on the money we were making. So I went back to school for hairdressing. Hairdressers made more money than mechanical engineers.

[So we] came here. My aunt came before us, she paid two hundred dollars for me. Actually, the Jewish community sponsored us. For three months, we lived free. The process of coming was very long. We stayed two weeks in Austria, then two months in Italy while all the papers were done.

When we arrived here, there was a school, there was money for rent. You can't bring anything out from Russia, nothing. My brother was in the Soviet Army and [we left] my parents. It was the hardest part.

From day one, we had to face the real world. You don't speak the language. You don't know what's going on around you. You're in a completely different world. There's nothing as difficult as this. I was comparing this to when the Germans expelled the Jews in World War II. They had to leave. We made the choice.

It was extremely difficult for my husband. There he was a man. Here, he doesn't speak the language, he's an idiot. He was working as a lab assistant. It was his first real job, and he was trying to get into some room and the door was locked and the students were laughing at him. Almost forty years old and he couldn't read the sign.

With my son, the community put him in a Jewish day school. It was a school for only Russian kids, learning English and Hebrew at the same time. He's a little kid, he speaks only Russian, everything is so confusing. And we had no religious background. In Russia, I was ashamed of my grandfather. He was religious, he had a Jewish name, Chaim. All my life I was told, "You're a Jew." But in Russia we didn't practice Judaism.

Looking back, I can analyse it now. American Jews expected too much of us back then. And we, we took the help we were getting as a given. We were used to being led, [having] no choice was a way of life. Coming here, again someone else was making choices. This is where you can live, this is what we're going to teach you. [Again] no choices. We didn't think to be grateful, we just accepted. We [thought] the government entitles you. I remember my aunt telling me, "Make sure they give you the thousand dollars." So the first question I asked through the interpreter was, "Am I getting my thousand dollars?" When I think back, I'm ashamed.

After three months, I went to school at a community college. I couldn't read very well, I couldn't write. So when I got an opportunity to study computers, I found programming much easier. [But] take the word "hardware," a popular computer word. You look it up in the dictionary, it says it's a store.

You can imagine! My husband is never home, he's working nights in a bagel shop, cash money. I have a little kid. I always wanted for my son more than I could give him so I'm working out of my house doing hairdressing. When he was eight, there was one toy in the house, no television, and no family I could leave him with. I didn't buy a bed. We were sleeping on the floor. Homework was the only thing he could do.

But now, my husband is a Ph.D., a tenured college professor teaching physical education and health. He had his master's from Russia and got his Ph.D. here.

Without the help of the Jewish community, it would have been much harder. They were giving us advice because we couldn't make our own decisions. There were counselors and all the assistance they gave was free. We would have survived, yes, but it would have taken much longer to become somebody.

In Russia, there was no such thing as practicing Judaism. I never knew what shabbos was. Here, from day one, I felt good, not being ashamed and actually being proud. In Russia, everything not Russian was Jewish. My maiden name was a very Jewish name, I was ashamed of that name, ashamed to say it. I was ashamed of my grandfather and grandmother speaking with accents, but I loved them to death. I remember Yom Kippur, they always had family around the table and my grandfather was dahvening [praying devoutly] and the kids were laughing at him. But we loved being there. We didn't understand any of it. But that was our family. We were ashamed and loving it at the same time.

I didn't change so fast here. When my son was telling me things they were teaching him in [religious] school, I was telling him to leave me alone. He said, "You don't eat pork and on Friday you have shabbos." I laughed. I feel sorry about this now, making fun of him. I made a big mistake by not encouraging him.

After two years of Jewish day school, we had to make a choice. The public school was pretty good and we didn't have to pay. He was never part of the group at the Jewish school, never invited to parties. We weren't on the same economic level. So we sent him to public school.

At that time we lived in a very Jewish neighborhood, so we knew to take off for Jewish holidays. [We saw] our neighbors dressed up, walking to shul. What are we doing? We are landscaping around the house. To us what is normal is to use your day off. Now I understand. Then? I thought it was my business what I do.

Now, it's different. Little by little we understand a lot about Judaism. We go to temple, we participate. We're still not religious, but we want to have our holidays, we want to be part of the community. Friends invited us to temple, people were friendly, they welcomed us. I was very sick, I had breast cancer and we decided to become members. Now we're there every Friday night. I don't know if God hears, but I pray and I feel good.

I always knew we'd have to work the rest of our life. Absolutely. For money. It was never a choice. In Russia, there is no rich family, unless you're in government. Since I was fourteen, I was working and I'll work til I die. Today I work at the Superior Court of New Jersey and I make more *money than my husband. Men don't like that. So he's working extra, a part-time job as a night manager at a health club. My son is now twenty-seven, gorgeous. He is a physical therapist.*

What I dream about is staying home. But I'd have nothing to do. My son has his own place. What I want to say is I think women shouldn't work. They should take care of their husband and children. This is how God made it to be. I want my husband to be able to support me. I [wanted] to have five chilren. But I limited my family because I had to work.

Coming here was lucky. I provided opportunities for my child and I'm happy my son grew up here. He was living with a non-Jewish girl four years and she was not for him. I told him what I thought. They didn't break up because of me, but I contributed. I don't understand intermarriage. You have to bring up kids one way, you can't practice both. My son now goes for bar mitzvah. At age twenty-seven! I want my son to marry a Jewish girl. I want Jewish grandchildren.

Last spring we celebrated our thirtieth anniversary. We had a huppa and a rabbi and we went on honeymoon back to Kiev. It was exactly how I expected. I didn't like anything. I spent thirty years there and nothing, nothing. Everyone left. Either here or to Israel.

Here, all our friends are Jewish. Even the [Russians] who came recently, who are not going to get where they want to get, they are not sorry. Here is freedom. Choices. Opportunity. It's just so much better.

NATASHA, committed to giving her child a better life in America, became a proud Jew only after she left Kiev. It was *assimilation* that transformed her into an American and a Jew.

For JOAN, *feminism* has been a way of life since she was a child. No great epiphanies. No wrenching journeys. No fears and shame. JOAN spoke her mind in high school and still speaks out as an ardent feminist. No waffling and no qualifying. She and Natasha are close in age, but they come from very different backgrounds.

Joan

JOAN, 52, was captured by politics when she was only a kid in eighth grade. Charming, well spoken, and politically astute, she might have become a U.S. senator herself. Instead, she spent sixteen years working behind the scenes for a famous senator whose name she asks me not to reveal.

With a B.A. from Douglas College, she became a committed feminist. She never planned to have children—a deal she laid out firmly when she married her husband, a successful businessman. However, today she is the proud mother of two daughters, one in college.

Observing the ironic outcome of some of her early decisions, she laughs at herself. Today she is deeply dedicated to feminist causes and civil rights.

Raised in a traditional Jewish home, she describes holidays as "families getting together, not religious." Her friends were Jewish but no one was bat mitzvahed or confirmed. So when her parents told her, at fourteen, she could not go out with a boy who wasn't Jewish, "I paid them back in spades. Anyone I could find: black, orange, Buddhist, Roman Catholic."

Yet she recalls the warmth of her extended family with her grandparents living downstairs. "Family was the source of social life and also emotional and intellectual sustenance."

She found little in synagogue life to attract her. "I didn't understand Hebrew, it was a mystery when to stand up and sit down. And it remained that way until [my] daughter's bat mitzvah when I took courses and got some sense of not being a total alien."

She is a slim, pretty woman with intense, dark eyes; a lively conversationalist, personable, and opinionated.

IN 1959, WHEN JFK was running for president, I was captivated and contacted Democratic headquarters. I was only thirteen, in eighth grade, so I stuffed and I mailed. I met him and I melted on the spot!

In tenth grade I joined the NAACP and I was in Washington for King's "I have a dream" speech. It was unbelievable to be part of it, belonging to something enormous and doing something positive for society. Such a rush! I had no clue Jim Crow existed until my grandfather in Florida told me we couldn't go to a "colored" movie. It was a seminal moment. Horrifying. And I cried. It wasn't the land of the free.

Throughout college I worked for candidates that interested me on a national level, not mayor or freeholder. It was early Vietnam and I worked on gubernatorial races as well as Senate and House. In college I marched on Washington; it was the beginning of protest marches.

I was a bit of a rebel. Under this veneer of polite Nice Jewish Girl, I was a pain in the rear end, [so] my family was delighted that my husband was a white Jewish guy.

But I have to tell you, in my heart of hearts, I don't think same-religion marriage is essential. I've said this to my daughters. Having more in common than less, is what matters. Having shared experiences makes life easier. Quite honestly, I think my children would be happier married to an Italian from New York than a Jew from Wyoming.

I don't care if [they] marry into the religion or not. Once I had children, I felt they had to understand what it means to be a Jew, so I took off for Jewish holidays. Both children went to private school and Hebrew school and they learned a great deal.

My first job out of college was at the Newark Public Library; I was going to be Philip Roth. Then I became a social worker for six years. All you needed then was a car and a B.A.

I was married seven years before I had children. I never really wanted children. I'm not a patient person, I didn't think I'd be a particularly good mother. My father, when he thought I did something wrong, took out his strap and hit me. Which I think is inhuman and I resolved I would never, ever, place myself in a position to harm a child and therefore would never have children. When I got married, it was with the understanding we would not have children. [My husband] never believed I meant it.

In 1977 I got a job I loved. I got to work on a senatorial campaign! Then my husband said, "I want a child." And I said, "Tough! You're married to the wrong person." I [went] to marriage counseling and I said I'd agree if. If I had full-time household help and if I didn't have to be home at three o'clock. All non-negotiable. And he called my bluff. I had never even baby sat, I didn't like kids.

My first daughter was born when I was thirty-three.

From the moment I got out of bed and knew I had conceived, it was the most exciting, thrilling, eagerly awaited event of my life! I committed to it with a full heart. My husband learned to change diapers, he ran carpools, and he took them to doctor appointments.

Almost three years later our second daughter was born. I went back to work six weeks after each baby and I had no guilt. None. I was working full time. I had a full-time live-in nanny and somebody to clean the house, [so] we were fine. Given how inexperienced I was, it was best for the children. I was relieved. It meant I was free to have the life I needed to have.

I truly cherish my children, I adore them. But I could not have done it full time every day of the week. I was not guilty about working. My work made them possible. I couldn't have had children [without] a job that I loved. The respect and gratification made me a better mother. At home as a full-time mom I would have wound up hospitalized with padded walls. The children were not possible without the job. That was the balance.

My husband was the primary breadwinner, my job was the gravy, so there were many times he'd say, "You take off." And I'd say, "No, you're your own boss, you take off." But with my job, there was no part time.

A lot of people who know me describe me as the first feminist. My feminist tendencies tend to be based on equality rather than anyone being better or more powerful than anyone else. I was captivated by Betty Friedan's book and I took my children to political rallies, especially for women. I remember a Carol Bellamy speech and stuffing envelopes for Elizabeth Holtzman and Bella Abzug. It was important for them to know that women could hold all jobs. Don't depend on someone else, certainly not a man. It's not fair or appropriate.

The roles I [balanced] as mother and worker were psychologically ben-eficial. I got a strong emotional high, [each role] feeds the other. I think I'm a more interesting person and a more compassionate person because one contributes to the other.

How did I balance it all?

I'm a very well organized person, you have to be. I was working ten, twelve, fourteen hours a day. Physically tired. But my children were reju-venating. My husband didn't complain. [However], the spouse who earns the most money holds the power.

I was with the senator sixteen years. For me, it's about doing the right thing and making the world a better place. That sounds hopelessly naive, but I truly believe people have an obligation to make a difference.

I feel I made a difference. Standing at the Tidal Basin and listening to Dr. King's "I have a dream" speech made me feel we all made a differ-ence. The same was true marching on Washington during the Vietnam war. So many people! It was incredibly empowering. It's exerting a collec-tive will for the good. When like-minded people have a goal and work to-gether, it's a wonderful feeling.

Feminists can empower themselves by becoming part of what they be-lieve in. By making a lot of money. By breaking the glass ceiling. More and more families where mommy has money at her disposal, will con-tinue those changes we fought for as feminists. The economic power women are gaining make[s] it impossible to slide back very far.

Feminism has also empowered men and opened possibilities for them that never existed before. A man can cry and be a househusband and not the breadwinner. Corporations have not been sensitive to this, but even-tually they're not going to have a choice. So many women in so many powerful positions, it won't be possible to do it wrong.

Women won't have to be supermoms. That idea will die. Both parents will do non-gender-related roles and a lot of gender problems will go away as we share and balance our [work/family] roles. Sharing parent-ing, sharing breadwinning, sharing errands, we're sharing emotional and intellectual time. My children were far better off for having a full-time working mother.

For some Jews it's still, the woman cares for the family and he provides the economic situation. That's a conflict in some Orthodox quarters [and] that will have to change. Orthodox Jews seem to be expanding. Some of the resurgence of interest in religion is terrifying as hell. People don't have neighborhoods anymore, families are [spread] all over the country. So religion is giving people a sense of belonging to a community. With so much lack of civility, religion gives people a sense of returning to morality. The more isolated people become working on computers, the more they're going to need places for emotional and spiritual contact.

I left my job three years ago. Why? It was time to leave and I was losing perspective. My oldest was entering high school and in four years she'd be gone. I wasn't going to miss her becoming an adult. Our children matter enormously to us. I made this choice because I needed time with them.

What do I do now? I teach water aerobics part time. No regrets. I was a U.S. Senate aide. As liaison, I dealt with government agencies. Why your mother didn't get her social security check. IRS forms. How to get into the military. I made the arrangements for the academy appointments the Senator made. It was a very rewarding job. But it was time to stop.

Some feminists choose not to marry. They remain single because they don't want to to depend on a man and they don't plan to have children. Other feminists, like Joan, insist that children are enriched by having a full-time working mother. They say that the women's movement has also empowered men and given them possibilities that never before existed.

Many Jewish working women embrace these ideas. Even those who do not choose to call themselves "feminists" respect many of these concepts. To detractors who claim that feminism has eroded Judaism, they answer, "Nonsense! Feminism has enhanced Jewish family life."

Professor Fishman's book *A Breath of Life* shows us clearly that feminism contributed to making our lives better. Indeed, many of the early feminist writers were Jewish women. In the 1970s, even while under the gun of hostile anti-Semitism at women's conferences, Jewish feminists refused to be shouted down. Being Jewish and feminist worked for them.

While traditional Jews insist that women need strict guidelines for every human pleasure, feminists continue to move ahead to revise and renew Jewish family life. They have enriched our vocabularies and forced us to face a gamut of social issues: job equality, equal pay, power and money, gender-related work, domestic equity, shared parenting, and domestic violence.

Indeed, much of American feminism flowed from a Jewish point of view. The concept of *tikkun olam*, the charge to repair the world, says Fishman, leads to "the attempt to defend the rights of oppressed groups, women, and minorities—the most vulnerable members of society."

Joan's interview demonstrates this. She says that feminism is about doing the right thing and making the world a better place. Feminism may be a way of secularizing our Jewish impulse: *tikkun olam*. If Jews are more political, more socialistic, more altruistic, more liberal, and more committed to civil rights, perhaps that is because Judaism preaches these values. To have *rachmones* (compassion) for the less fortunate and to practice *tsedakka* via acts of charity are Jewish values we honor.

Valerie Gay, portfolio manager for PNC Advisors in Philadelphia, says women own about eight million businesses in the United States and collectively earn more than one trillion dollars per year. More than half of all married women make 50 percent or more of their family's income. Single women head nearly 40 percent of all households. That's economic power. The reality is that about 85 percent of women, *at some point in their lives*, will be responsible for managing their own finances.

Some Jews, fearful of assimilation and feminism, are crying out, "Oh my God, what happened to Judaism?" For Natasha, assimilation translated to becoming a Jew and joining a temple. Once ashamed of being Jewish, Natasha now wants her son to marry a Jew. Some women still insist you can't have it all, best to stay home and raise your kids.

Others like Joan claim that you can work and raise decent kids and have a happy Jewish home too. There are statistics on each side. But few can deny that we are living closer to a feminist point of view.

Feminism has made its mark and Judaism's legacy is now felt worldwide. Feminists in Iran, in China, and in Africa are having their say and enlightening their cultures.

As more Jewish working women meet culturally diverse people in the workplace, ideas are bound to be exchanged. These forces—assimilation and feminism—will redefine family life and redesign the workplace.

Throughout these chapters you've heard many women and many voices. Tales of sorrow and tales of joy. Dreams dashed and dreams fulfilled. Tough times and good times. Pain and courage.

What conclusions can we draw?

In the final chapter, we pull these threads together.

12

CONCLUSIONS

What themes stand out in the complicated lives of Jewish working women? How are we different from other working women who are engaged in the daily challenges of balancing work and love? And how are we just like them?

Jews are Democrats and Republicans, *shomar shabbat* and Saturday mall rats, deeply spiritual and blatantly materialistic. What can we conclude? Our diversity is a direct reflection of how Jewish we feel in America and how American we feel being Jewish. We respond to these two cultural imperatives. Sometimes they are in sync, sometimes not. The voices of these Jewish working women show where Jewish and American values dovetail and where they part company. They also reveal divergent opinions on the value of work, self-sacrifice, and religious ritual. The feelings, conflicts, and desires of these women spotlight the volatile conjunction of work, family, and religious life at the millennium, and sometimes offer a path for the future.

I have divided the conclusions into religious issues, love and family issues, and work issues. Work issues outnumber the others, but as you shall see, themes resonate from section to section. This overlap shows how work has infiltrated the home, how family issues have invaded the workplace, and how a Jewish religious sensibility guides our response to an unprecedented reshaping of American life.

Religious Issues

ISSUE 1. Jewish working women are keenly aware of themselves as Jews. Even if they are not observant of *kashruth* (laws about Kosher foods) or sabbath, they identify as Jews and take off from work as a sign of respect for the Jewish holidays. Many do this to send a message to their children: Mom and Dad work very hard, but we also honor our heritage and our history. Although we don't adhere to all the laws, we are Jews. We expect you to value that.

ISSUE 2. Many working women are making the effort to see that their children are educated in Hebrew schools, Jewish day schools, and synagogues. Bar and bat mitzvah are regarded as part of Jewish life, as is confirmation. For Jewish working mothers, adding yet another obligatory carpool is no fun. But their children's Jewish education is important. One effect is that the children draw the parents back to the synagogue. Some enroll in adult education courses and learn Hebrew. Their children's exposure has exposed *them*. My daughter-in-law Roni, who was not bat mitzvahed as a child, studied for her bat mitzvah while a working mother of two small children.

ISSUE 3. Divorced women report that synagogues are not responsive to their needs once the marriage breaks up. Also, lesbian women find synagogues and community centers less than welcoming. Intermarried women voice the same complaint. These groups have special needs which the Jewish community is not addressing. They need support. They need information. They need resources. The search for spirituality sometimes leads Jews away from Judaism to other religions. Unless Judaism becomes more inclusive, more and more Jews will abandon it. Synagogues that unite us help us reclaim our spirituality. This revitalization is sorely needed.

ISSUE 4. Synagogues that employ women as rabbis, cantors, *mohels*, administrators, and leaders, give Jewish women a vital affirmative message. Excluding women from roles of Jewish leadership is reprehensible. Jewish woman are taken seriously in the American workforce. Exclusion in the religious workforce is grievous and alienating. Synagogues that address this imbalance restore women's faith in Judaism's fairness and tap a rich source of female leaders.

ISSUE 5. Deeply embedded in Judaism is the Jewish Mother message: above all, we must be good mothers. Anything that compromises that duty is judged harshly, and the Jewish woman who puts her work above her children is harshly criticized. Most working women say that some measure of guilt comes with the territory. The clash between Judaism's dedicated dutiful mother and America's upwardly mobile working mom is the issue we wrestle with every day. However, we are balancing work and love with increasing efficiency and decreasing guilt, convinced we are better mothers because we work.

ISSUE 6. Many women recalled a trip to Israel as powerfully transformative, reconnecting them to Judaism. With the alienation of young Jews from their heritage, one solution proposed is to send Jewish youths to Israel to strengthen their identity and deepen their ties. Some organizations are proposing free trips underwritten by Jewish philanthropists. Will it work?

ISSUE 7. As incivility and violence increasingly define American culture, we see more and more people seeking solace in spiritual healing. With so many of us on short fuses, religion may become a crucial antidote to the hurried madness of everyday life. Jewish values and Jewish spirituality offer one such oasis. While Americans will never return to the sweet innocence portrayed in Norman Rockwell paintings, synagogue life may refresh us, offering relief from stress and moments to sit and reflect.

ISSUE 8. With synagogue attendance and affiliation declining, and the number of women in the workplace increasing, Judaism can not ignore the changing nature of the Jewish family. Ritual may attract some Jewish families. However, other families, hungry for spirituality and meaning, need to drink from another well: the poetry and beauty of Jewish values.

Love and Family Issues

ISSUE 1. Where American culture and Jewish culture collide most sharply is not in the office but in the home. Once wives used to ask their husbands' permission before going to work. Today, many husbands expect their wives to share the job of breadwinner. Few women can afford to stay home. Wives have become partners in the financial responsibility of raising a family. This requires adjustments, trade-offs, and creative compromises within family life.

ISSUE 2. Working women are no longer willing to carry out domestic tasks alone: they expect their spouse to do his fair share. Men, with kids in tow, are pushing supermarket carts, emptying dishwashers, and preparing meals. True, most women wind up doing the lion's share, but arrangements are often based on timeframes, workloads, school buses, commuter traffic, and what makes sense. Today's working women expect men to share in childrearing. Teamwork is the goal.

ISSUE 3. Stress is the major complaint of dual-career families. Working wives' chief problem is exhaustion, with no time to recharge their batteries. Too rushed to accomplish it all. Too tired for sex. Too stressed to relate to their husband as lover and best friend. To do her job and sustain a loving relationship with her family is the overwhelming challenge of the working woman.

ISSUE 4. Jewish mothers are demanding mothers. Why? Jews value education. America preaches competitiveness, encourages us to root for winners, and urges us to admire millionaires. We push our children early, we rush them from dance competitions to sports play-offs, producing overprogrammed kids who are as stressed out as their parents. Ten-year-olds stay in touch via cell phones. At Harvard, 20 percent of undergraduates are Jewish, though Jews are only 2 percent of the overall population. In the race for overachievers, are Jewish families raising healthy children?

ISSUE 5. When divorce occurs, the single working mom faces the double whammy of raising her children alone and living with diminished financial resources. She feels guilty and angry. Result? Her working life becomes both a burden and a comfort. It is a burden to be the major or sole breadwinner. It is a comfort to escape to the office where her work is appreciated and her damaged self-esteem is restored. For some divorced women, the workplace offers the solace and sociability of a family.

ISSUE 6. Despite the shortage of time, working women maintain friendships with other women. Under stress they reach for their women friends. They boost and console each other in an atmosphere of trust. For some working women, friends and colleagues in the workplace are as important as their husbands for emotional support. In general, Jewish women maintain strong bonds with other women.

ISSUE 7. Working women have tasted the power of money, and they love it. Money confers independence and freedom. It offers an array of options. In her book *Deborah, Golda and Me*, Letty Cottin Pogrebin says that "power is the ultimate weapon when the name of the game is How To Not Be a Footstool as a Woman and a Jew." However, a wife's power can be a problem for her husband if he is used to calling the tune. If she outearns him, the power shifts.

ISSUE 8. In some homes, a Mr. Mom is created when the male partner is willing to be the househusband. This restructures the family in ways our parents could never have imagined. The husband becomes the nurturer, the wife the breadwinner. Husbands are finding a new sense of purpose in raising children and they value that work.

ISSUE 9. Sex. Who has time for it? As working families shuttle from one appointment to another, each obligation takes on a priority, and sex is last on the list. Couple time diminishes. Many women say they have good marriages, but there's just no time to spend on the couple relationship. Is this kicking the divorce rate up?

ISSUE 10. Working families raising children will add yet another stress in the coming years: how to care for aging parents. According to the U.S. Bureau of the Census, hundredth birthdays will lose their mystique. Americans could face the burden of 4.2 million elderly by the year 2050. How working women behave toward their own parents and in-laws could become the most important challenge of the millennium. Because women turn out to be the caretakers of the elderly, they will decide how to obey the Mosaic injunction to honor your mother and father.

ISSUE 11. The cost of raising a family has shot way up. The list of what families need, or think they need, has swelled. Malls offer designer clothes for infants, school kids rack up frequent-flier miles, and more and more consumer goods are labeled "Kosher for Passover." Wants have turned into needs. Are Jewish working families going crazy? Have we bought into a "bottom line" American ethos that greed is good? American materialism has invaded Jewish homes. The more we work, the more we need to work.

ISSUE 12. The Jewish working woman often turns to her own mother for help in a crunch. Forget the myth of the overbearing, overcritical Jewish mother. As adults, women seem very much attached to their own mothers. They call on them in an emergency and Jewish grandparents pitch in with love and money. Even families scattered by thousands of miles call on each other. Many Jewish women are intensely attached to their mothers.

ISSUE 13. Alcoholism, drug use, adultery, gambling, domestic violence, and even incest, long considered by Jews to be the "problems of Gentiles," have invaded Jewish homes. Shameful behavior among Jews is more common than we think. Are we "a light unto the nations"? Or have we succumbed to the same destructive behaviors we once dismissed as not a Jewish problem? While Jewish Family Services responds to families in need, Judaism itself appears to offer little immunity against these problems.

ISSUE 14. Divorced parents, however hard they try to relieve their children's pain, often end up in ugly litigation and in custody battles. Children of divorce may pay long-term emotional costs and may feel that marriage is unworkable. Divorced mothers worry that their example has soured their unmarried adult children about marriage and children.

ISSUE 15. Young single women are having a hard time finding Jewish mates. To that end they are using personal columns, JCC and synagogue programs, the Internet—whatever promises results. Jewish matchmakers, trying to stem the tide of intermarriages, have come back into the picture offering high-tech, data-based searches to attract Jewish mates. However, as singles hit the forty mark, they may decide to widen the pool to include non-Jewish husbands. At a certain point, marrying Jewish may be compromised.

Work Issues

ISSUE 1. Employers are increasingly aware that many of their female employees are balancing work and families. To ignore this costs money, so women are taken more seriously. Most companies are not interested in empowering women, make no mistake about that. They simply do not want to lose excellent workers. Family-friendly workplaces are increasing because employers see that family issues are workplace issues. Companies that support families enhance their firm's productivity.

ISSUE 2. The American workplace has hastened assimilation, secularization, and intermarriage. "Around the year 2025, Caucasians will no longer make up a majority of the country's population," says J. Michael Adams, president of Fairleigh Dickinson University. As Jewish working women mingle with non-Jewish and non-Caucasian colleagues, reevaluation of some personal goals are bound to occur.

ISSUE 3. Volunteer work for Jewish organizations has fallen off sharply among working women who can't cram another activity into their schedules. Until Jewish leaders come up with tactics to attract younger women, volunteerism will remain the domain of older women, retired women, and wealthy women. The increase in the number of Jewish working women has changed the very nature of Jewish philanthropies.

ISSUE 4. Workaholics are increasing among Jewish mothers. Lured by large salaries and exciting work, they depend on grandparents, husbands, and nannies to balance their family and worklife. They are surprisingly guilt free and believe their children are well cared for.

ISSUE 5. Some women switch to part-time work when they return from maternity leave. To them it feels like the right adjustment to balancing work and love. Shocked by the intensity of the mother-child bond, they want to be responsible caregivers in their child's life. Some women even juggle several part-time jobs to fit around their family life.

ISSUE 6. Working women need flexibility. That means returning to work when they feel ready. The route may be part time for six months, then back to full time. Other alternatives are working from home, less "face" time, and less reporting to the office. Employers who measure a woman's productivity instead of her time in the office are likelier to maintain a loyal female staff.

ISSUE 7. Some women go part time after a child arrives, as a temporary segue before resuming full time. However, for others the choice is part time for a long time, perhaps until their children are in high school. The price tag for this comes high: loss of wages, loss of respect, loss of skills. Dropping out of the full-time workforce, they lose their status as serious contenders worthy of promotions.

ISSUE 8. Some working women who can afford it just quit cold turkey once their child—or, more commonly, their second child— comes along. They yearn to be stay-at-home moms and they won't turn over childrearing to anyone else. They want to share the precious years of their children's growing up. Perhaps they feel more guilt than others Jewish mothers. Perhaps work becomes less satisfying. For them, quitting is not a sacrifice, it is a positive choice.

ISSUE 9. Most women work out a plan that lets them be maximally productive at work and active players in their children's lives. They go to the school plays, the baseball games, and the doctors' appointments. Parenting is their first priority. Practical women, they shift gears when necessary to achieve a good balance. My daughter Lisa, a CPA, does some of her work at home where she can keep an eye on the kids.

ISSUE 10. Women, more often than men, are the peacemakers. We absorb stress at home, we discipline the kids, and we "make nice" in family squabbles. Stress in the workplace added to family stress knocks us off balance. Therefore, some women choose no-brainer jobs, employers who don't hassle, commutes that don't exhaust, and supervisors who are not perfectionists. More important than money and status is a less stressful job.

ISSUE 11. Many women do phasing, or sequencing, to balance work and love. At one point in their worklife they are committed to moving up. Later, they switch to mothering while their children are small and needy. At another phase, they may return to school or change jobs. Mindful of their family obligations, Jewish working women enter and leave the workforce, phasing in and out. Time to forge ahead. Time to nurture. Time to step off. Time to return. Phasing provides a comfort level to balancing work and love.

ISSUE 12. While most women enjoy their jobs, savoring the self-esteem and empowerment, they are also aware of the deglamorization of work. Just getting out of the house, a motivation for many in the 1970s and 1980s, no longer carries the same weight. Work produces its own stress. Having a job is not sufficient validation unless the job fits in with family life. The potential glamour of some work does not blind women to the pressures of the daily balancing act.

ISSUE 13. The major issue facing working mothers is finding quality childcare. Unless they are satisfied that their children are well cared for, their work suffers. Childcare provided by on-site locations or arranged privately must give them peace of mind. Jewish working mothers declare over and over that their children come first. That's their priority. Most don't believe in "quality time." An hour crammed in before bedtime does not make up for inadequate childcare.

ISSUE 14. With more women at executive levels, corporations are changing. This rise in power promotes work/family issues that reflect the woman's point of view. We have moved away from a society built on physical power. Today it's brain power and communication power, in which many women excel. Companies that promote talented women are forced to face family issues as never before.

ISSUE 15. Young women expect to work and also to raise children. But here's an interesting development: The work ethic is changing. Men are not as career driven as they used to be. They want to be good fathers, involved with their kids' lives. Result? Family life is changing the workplace because men are changing, too.

ISSUE 16. Women are asking about a company's culture before they sign on. They are interviewing the interviewer and selecting corporations that are rated high in family categories. *Working Mother* publishes a list of one hundred best companies and rates them on issues such as childcare, flexibility, advancement of women, and parental leave. Women are choosing their workplace based on balancing work and family life.

ISSUE 17. Workplaces are using e-mail, videoconferencing, voice mail and hotlines to schools to accomodate their employees. Women who ask for on-the-job options are getting more support. Technology is changing the hierarchy of many workplaces, making it easier for women (and men) to be good parents.

ISSUE 18. Having It All is possible. To an extent. Perfect kids? Perfect job? Perfect marriage? Only in your dreams. Despite illness, divorce, money presures, job loss, and personal tragedy, balancing jobs and families is possible. Jewish working women tell us that work and love provide a rich life. Not easy. But doable.

Both the American dream and the Jewish dream are alive and well. Today, Jewish women are feminists and traditionalists, secular and Orthodox, workaholics and full-time moms. Coping with families and work takes many forms and invites many choices.

You've heard their stories. You've seen how balancing work and love is difficult. But Jewish women are resilient. Having a family doesn't stop them. They accept challenging jobs, change priorities, phase in and out of the workforce, and flip careers. Mindful that their number one priority is family, they tell us that they bring Jewish values to the workforce.

The good news is that this struggle is moving us toward a more collaborative society. Employers are really listening to women and accommodating them. Against the odds, women in the workforce have humanized corporations. And Jewish working women have had an incalculable impact. We are not diffident and intimidated. We are movers and shakers.

In the challenge to balance work and love, traditional Jewish values may be compromised or altered, but they are not easily dismissed from our consciousness. Our Jewish history and destiny continue to inform our choices. We are not merely working women, we are Jewish working women. We have changed the workplace and family life. Some say for the worse. I think for the better!

Today's workforce is made up of married women, single mothers, step-mothers, grandmothers, step-grandmothers, lesbians, divorced women, separated women, singles, entrepreneurs, CEOs, doctors, astronauts, senators—the list is long. Work and love, both essential ingredients, make our daily lives possible and impossible. As Jewish working women, our rich heritage and commitment to social justice have accelerated many changes in the American workforce.

You have heard a rich variety of voices. Pain and joy. Frustration and success. Our task now as Jewish working women is to forge stronger partnerships with our husbands and employers. To create strong Jewish families. To enjoy both satisfying work and loving family life. To raise mensches and be mensches.

Work and love will continue to change us, both empower us and humanize the workplace. We cannot predict the future. But we can count on some things: The social consequences of more sophisticated technology will create new challenges that we cannot foresee. Medical advances will set new goals for a rich, long life. What is clear is that while we are busy solving the daily challenges of balancing work and love, new challenges will arise.

Work will change. Families will change. Judaism will change. Will we find solutions? Of course we will.

Jewish working women are unstoppable! I can't wait to see the next generation in action. I can't wait to see how my grandchildren change the world.

Bibliography for Further Reading

Antler, Joyce, ed. *Talking Back: Images of Jewish Women in American Popular Culture.* Hanover, N.H.: University Press of New England/Brandeis University Press, 1997.

Barnett, Rosalind C., and Caryl Rivers. *He Works, She Works: How Two Income Families Are Happier, Healthier, and Better Off.* San Francisco: Harper, 1996.

Baum, Charlotte; Paula Hyman; and Sonya Michel. *The Jewish Woman in America.* New York: New American Library, 1976.

Cardoza, Arlene. *Sequencing.* New York: Collier Books/Macmillan Publishing, 1986.

Chira, Susan. *A Mother's Place: Taking the Debate About Working Mothers Beyond Guilt and Blame.* New York: HarperCollins, 1998.

Costello, Cynthia, and Barbara Kivimae Krimgold, eds. *The American Woman (1996–97) Women & Work.* New York: Norton, 1996.

Crosby, Faye J. *Juggling: The Unexpected Advantages of Balancing Career and Home for Women and Their Families.* New York: Free Press, 1991.

Davidson, Sara. *Cowboy.* New York: HarperCollins, 1999.

Faludi, Susan. *Backlash: The Undeclared War Against American Women.* New York: Crown Publishers, 1991.

Farber, Roberta Rosenberg, and Chaim I. Waxman, eds. *Jews in America: A Contemporary Reader.* Hanover, N.H.: University Press of New England/Brandeis University Press, 1999.

Fishman, Sylvia Barack. *A Breath of Life: Feminism in the American Jewish Community.* New York: The Free Press, 1993.

Friedan, Betty. *The Feminine Mystique.* New York: Norton, 1963; reprint, 1983.

Glenn, Susan A. *Daughters of the Shtetl: Life and Labor in the Immigrant Generation.* Ithaca and London: Cornell University Press, 1990.

Goldstein, Rebecca. *The Mind-Body Problem.* New York: Dell Publishing, 1985.

Gordis, Robert. *Love and Sex: A Modern Jewish Perspective.* New York: Farrar, Straus & Giroux, 1978.

Gornick, Vivian. *Fierce Attachments.* New York: Farrar, Straus & Giroux, 1987.

Greenberg, Blu. *On Women and Judaism: A View from Tradition.* Philadelphia: The Jewish Publication Society of America, 1981.

Hartman, Moshe, and Harriet Hartman. *Gender Equality and American Jews.* Albany: State University of New York Press, 1996.

Heilbrun, Carolyn. *Writing a Woman's Life.* New York: Ballantine, 1989.

Hochschild, Arlie Russell. *The Time Bind: When Work Becomes Home and Home Becomes Work.* New York: Metropolitan Books/Henry Holt, 1997.

Holcomb, Betty. *Not Guilty: The Good News about Working Mothers.* New York: Scribner, 1998.

Hyman, Paula E. *Gender and Assimilation in Modern Jewish History.* Seattle: University of Washington Press, 1995.

Hyman, Paula E., and Deborah Dash Moore. *Jewish Women in America.* New York: Schocken Books, 1987.

Kessler-Harris, Alice. *Out of Work: A History of Wage-Earning Women in the United States.* New York: Oxford University Press, 1982.

Koltun, Elizabeth, ed. *The Jewish Woman: An Anthology.* New York: Schocken Books, 1987.

Kuzmack, Linda Gordon, and George Saloman. *Working and Mothering: A Study of 97 Jewish Career Women with Three or More Children.* New York: National Jewish Family Center of the American Jewish Committee, 1980.

McKenna, Elizabeth Perle. *When Work Doesn't Work Anymore: Women, Work and Identity.* New York: Delacorte Press, 1997.

Nadell, Pamela S. *Women Who Would Be Rabbis.* Boston: Beacon Press, 1998.

Peters, Joan K. *When Mothers Work: Loving Our Children Without Sacrificing Ourselves.* Reading, Mass.: Addison-Wesley, 1997.

Pogrebin, Letty Cottin. *Deborah, Golda and Me.* New York: Crown, 1991.

Schwartz, Felice N. *Breaking with Tradition: Women and Work, the New Facts of Life.* New York: Warner Books, 1992.

Shor, Juliet B. *The Overworked American.* New York: Basic Books, 1991.

Simmons, Howard. *Jewish Times.* Boston: Houghton Mifflin, 1988.

Sklare, Marshall. *America's Jews.* New York: Random House, 1971.

Steinem, Gloria. *Moving Beyond Words.* New York: Simon & Schuster, 1994.

Swiss, Deborah J., and Judith P. Walker. *Women and the Work/Family Dilemma.* New York: John Wiley, 1993.

Werthheimer, Jack. *A People Divided.* Hanover, N.H.: University Press of New England/Brandeis University Press, 1997.

Wetherby, Terry, ed. *Conversations: Working Women Talk about Doing a "Man's Job."* Millbrae, Calif.: Les Femmes, 1977.